STUDY SKILLS *for* PSYCHOLOGY

STUDY SKILLS *for* PSYCHOLOGY

Succeeding in Your Degree

Richard P.J. Freeman and Tony Stone

⑤SAGE Publications

London ● Thousand Oaks ● New Delhi

First published 2006

SAGE Publications Ltd
1 Oliver's Yard
55 City Road
London EC1Y 1SP

SAGE Publications Inc.
2455 Teller Road
Thousand Oaks, California 91320

SAGE Publications India Pvt Ltd
B-42, Panchsheel Enclave
Post Box 4109
New Delhi 110 017

British Library Cataloguing in Publication data

A catalogue record for this book is available
from the British Library

ISBN-10 0-7619-4239-4   ISBN-13 978-0-7619-4239-9
ISBN-10 0-7619-4240-8   ISBN-13 978-0-7619-4240-5 (pbk)

Library of Congress Control Number: 2005935708

Typeset by C&M Digitals (P) Ltd., Chennai, India
Printed and bound in Great Britain by TJ International Ltd, Padstow, Cornwall
Printed on paper from sustainable resources

Dedication

This book is dedicated to Richard's parents, Gordon and Joyce, and to the memory of Tony's parents, Jack and Gwen.

Contents

About the Authors

Richard P.J. Freeman, PhD, MA (Cantab.), is Coordinator of Generic Skills and Data Analysis at the Institute of Education, University of London. He is a member of the British Psychological Society's Graduate Qualifications Accreditation Committee and the International Committee. Richard is also secretary general and vice-president of the European Federation of Psychologists' Associations.

Tony Stone, MA, BA (Hons), is a principal lecturer at London South Bank University where he is the course director for the graduate diploma in psychology and teaches conceptual and historical issues in psychology and cognitive science. His main interests are in the philosophy of mind and psychology. He is on the editorial board of the journal *Mind and Language.*

1 Introduction

How this Book Works

Psychology is a broad and diverse subject. On your degree course you will find that you have to master material which ranges from the hard science that comprises contemporary psychobiology to the more interpretative skills required in some areas of social and cultural psychology. You will be trained to use a range of research methods: experiments, interviews, questionnaires and the rest. Alongside this you will need to know how to manipulate and interpret the data that these methods generate. You will find that you will need to write in a variety of different formats: essays and practical reports primarily, but you might also have to produce posters, leaflets and bibliographies. This diversity is challenging.

This book is designed to help you to meet these challenges by introducing you to a range of study skills and providing you with ways to practise those skills.

This book is structured around three basic themes: *Organisation*, *Communication* and *Reflection* (OCR). We aim to provide you with advice and guidance on how you can develop the skills you need to be organised in order to communicate your ideas effectively and to understand what others are trying to communicate to you. As you will see, an important part of the development of these skills is continual reflection on what you have achieved with the aim of improved future performance. You will get more out of every facet of your course if you can develop these skills. For example, you will attend a large number of lectures during your time at university, as they are major vehicles for the delivery of the knowledge you need to become a psychologist. We will show you in Chapter 5 how to make the most of lectures. But in essence it comes down to this. A lecture is where a psychology tutor will *communicate* with you. You need to be *organised* to get the most out of a lecture, and in this context this means you have to be prepared. After the lecture you should *reflect* on what you have learned so that you put that knowledge to good use in other teaching situations and, of course, in your essays and examinations. In our experience, students who struggle in their studies do so because they are inadequately organised, are unreflective, and so fail to get the most out of what lecturers are trying to communicate to them. These students do less well than they are able as they fail to communicate their ideas to lecturers, which results in frustration in seminars and low marks in assessments.

Personal Development Planning (PDP)

PDP is a process in which all university students are now required to participate. The objective is to provide students with a framework through which they can understand what and how they learn, and to enable them to plan, review and take responsibility for their own learning, performance and achievements. Throughout your course, therefore, you will be asked to reflect on the skills you are developing that will help you with your career once you leave, whether or not this is in the area of professional psychology. It is expected that this will help you when applying for jobs or further courses of study.

You will be required to develop and maintain a personal development record (PDR) that should include:

- **A personal record of your learning and achievement (provided by the university).**

- **A skills checklist and personal plan completed by you at the beginning of the course and updated regularly so that you can monitor your progress throughout the course.**

- **Reflective self-evaluation of your personal input to each semester's units.**

As PDP is a new initiative it is impossible to say now how it is likely to be introduced on your degree course. However, it should become clear as you read through this book that the skills you learn, especially those based around the OCR themes, are exactly what you require to get the most out of the PDP process.

How to Use this Book

We encourage you to read this book straight through when you first buy it, so you get a basic idea of what it contains and the skills you need to acquire in order to succeed on your psychology degree. But skills are acquired over time with practice, not all at once, so you should expect to turn to this book time and time again. The book should accompany you throughout your degree course, as it is a resource that you can use whenever you need help. For example, when you have to write a coursework essay, it should be part of your preparation to re-read the section of this book that deals with essay writing, and do again the exercises we suggest. You might then reflect on the extent to which you followed our advice in previous essays, and how you might do so more thoroughly this time around. We want to stress right at the beginning, however, that we are providing advice and guidance on how to study, not rigid rules that can be thoughtlessly applied. The major message of this book is that you need to take control of your studies if you are to succeed. You can begin to do this if you use this book as an aid to develop for yourself the method of study that works for you.

We have tried to break the text up with various features that should help you to identify the learning content of each chapter. The learning outcomes placed in a box at the beginning of each chapter highlight what you should have learned by its end. Examples and illustrations provide concrete exemplification of the major study skills that each chapter discusses. Exercises and learning aids are there to enable you to practise important skills. It is important that you complete the exercises and use the learning aids as you will not get full benefit from this book unless you use it actively to develop your skills.

What You will Find in this Book

In Chapter 2 we provide a very brief overview of the nature of a psychology degree. We also give you advice about what you need to sort out in the first few weeks of university and what to do when things go wrong. In Chapter 3 we talk about 'Managing Yourself and Others'. You might think that's unusual for a study skills book, but it's actually the most important skill for success in a psychology degree. While intelligence is required for success on a psychology degree, good organisation is essential to get the most out of the intelligence you possess. It is essential that you take control of your learning and this chapter will help you to do that.

In Chapter 4 we outline how you go about 'Doing Psychology'. We begin by explaining the scientific method, which sounds a bit intimidating but actually just explains what we are trying to do as psychologists when we examine behaviour and cognition. We also look at how research can help us to increase our knowledge and understanding of psychology. In particular, we focus on the key things you need to understand – and be able to report – about statistics.

In Chapter 5 we focus on 'Teaching Situations' such as lectures, seminars and tutorials, and discuss how you can get the most out of each of these by appropriate preparation and follow-up. In Chapter 6 we provide a brief overview of the various 'Assessments' that you will have during your degree and outline various ways in which you can improve your marks. In Chapter 7 we discuss 'Using Resources Effectively' and highlight how you can use the Internet and other electronic resources as well as books and journal papers.

In Chapter 8 we help you with 'The Psychology Project' or dissertation. In particular, we help you to come up with a good project idea. 'Good' means that your idea should be feasible for an undergraduate project, that is, that you can complete it in the time allocated, that you have access to the appropriate resources (including participants) and that it is ethically sound. In the final chapter, 'Future Directions', we outline the various career paths available to psychologists. It is important to read this chapter as soon as possible, since to be able to follow your preferred career path in psychology it is very useful to have done relevant work experience or to have chosen particular units of study. Finally, there is an Index so you can find information about particular tasks or ideas more easily.

Note on Referencing

As this is a study skills book and not a scholarly monograph or a journal article, we have not provided reference lists at the end of chapters or at the end of the book. We thought it would be more helpful to the reader to include the full reference of any study we refer to within the text itself.

Final Introductory Words

Psychology is great fun. People are complex and it is fascinating to try to figure out why and how they do what they do. It is a shame, therefore, when students struggle and don't enjoy their study. Reading this book will give you the skills to enjoy your time studying for and succeeding in your psychology degree.

2 So You Want to Do a Psychology Degree?

LEARNING OUTCOMES

1. To be aware of the basic structure of a psychology degree.
2. To understand the value of a psychology degree accredited by the British Psychological Society.
3. To be organised so that you get the most from the first few weeks and subsequent weeks of your psychology degree.
4. To understand how this book will help you to get the most out of your psychology degree.

Introduction

There is an enormous range of degree subjects currently available and each year there are further weird and wonderful subjects on offer. What then is psychology? A common reaction when you tell someone that you're a psychologist is 'I'd better be careful about what I say!' or 'Are you analysing me right now?'. But, in fact, psychology is not psychoanalysis. Psychoanalysis is a broad term that originates from the work of Sigmund Freud, though it is now split into numerous, often competing, schools of thought and practice. It can usefully be understood as centred on the idea of there being a 'talking cure' for psychological problems of various kinds. Psychology should also be clearly distinguished from psychiatry. Psychiatry is a branch of medicine and, in contrast to psychoanalysis, might usefully be thought of as centred on the idea that psychological problems have a 'chemical cure'.

Literally, psychology means 'study of the mind', but most psychologists would probably prefer to describe it as 'the science of the mind' with the focus on understanding human behaviour. One of Britain's leading psychologists, Professor Michael Eysenck, has described psychology as 'the science which uses introspective and behavioural evidence to understand the internal processes which lead people to think and to behave as they do' (Psychology is usually thought of as a science because it has relied on the scientific method to study the mind. We'll be explaining exactly what the scientific method is in Chapter 4, but in essence it means that we devise and carry out empirical studies to test our ideas: (hypotheses).

It is sometimes said that psychology is a young discipline but an old subject. On the one hand, the academically organised scientific investigation of the mind is little more than 125 years old but, on the other hand, the questions it addresses have interested people for thousands of years. For example: How do animals and people learn? Why do some people develop mental health problems? How do children learn language? These are all questions for psychology and are united by their focus on human and animal behaviour – 'What makes them tick?' is one way of thinking about it.

But is psychology anything more than common sense? Our 'common sense' tells us both that 'birds of a feather flock together' and 'opposites attract'. We need psychology to help us harness our common sense to enable us to understand human and animal behaviour, ideally so we can improve people's lives.

Why Do a Degree in Psychology?

You will have your own reasons for being interested in psychology. Over the years, we have met students with a wide variety of reasons for wanting to do a psychology degree. For example, we have had students who wanted to do psychology because they had helped care for a child on the autistic spectrum and wanted to understand autism. We have taught students who have had personal experience of mental health issues and wanted greater understanding of the causes and possible treatments. We have also taught students who have a clear idea of their career path and want to do psychology so that they can get a worthwhile and satisfying job. Why are you interested in psychology? You might have no clear idea of what you want to do, but just have an interest in the subject. These are all good reasons to do a degree in psychology.

It is important to stress that completing a psychology degree does not qualify you to practise as a chartered psychologist. A psychology degree provides you with the essential knowledge and skills in psychology to be eligible for the further postgraduate study that is required to become a chartered psychologist. You should note, however, that a psychology degree only does this if it is recognised by the British Psychology Society as leading to the Graduate Basis for Registration (GBR).

You Really Need Your Degree to Have 'GBR'

GBR stands for the Graduate Basis for Registration and means that the British Psychological Society (BPS) has accredited the degree. Most degrees in psychology are accredited by the BPS, but it is important to check before you start your degree; you can do so using the BPS website (www.bps.org.uk) or by asking the admissions tutor of the psychology department. For a course to be accredited and hence have GBR, the ratio of teaching staff to students must be no more than 1:20. It is not unusual in some other subjects for that ratio to be much higher, so a degree with GBR means that there will be more staff available for teaching. In addition, the BPS ensures that psychology degrees with GBR have appropriate laboratory facilities, appropriate access to relevant literature, and that the degree covers an appropriate range of material to an appropriate standard. Note that a course allowing graduate membership of the BPS is not the same as having GBR, so ensure you look for *GBR*.

Most importantly, having GBR means that you will be able to continue on after your degree to study on accredited post-graduate training programmes that will enable you to become a practising psychologist and be eligible for the BPS Register of Chartered Psychologists. That status is compulsory for some careers and so is not optional if you want to work in certain jobs. So you can see that there are real advantages in choosing a psychology degree with GBR.

In the final chapter we give details of careers that are possible for someone with a degree in psychology. If you are not familiar with the possible careers available to psychology graduates, it is a good idea to read through that final chapter sooner rather than later as it will help guide you in making choices for your university and non-university life. You will probably find the careers listed to be fascinating, but if you don't you may want to reflect on whether a psychology degree is the best degree for you. However, even if you are not planning to go on to be a practising psychologist, a psychology degree is an excellent preparation for subsequent work or study. On a psychology degree you develop writing skills, numerical and IT skills, and skills to investigate the real world that are eagerly sought after by employers.

What is the Structure of a Psychology Degree?

There is a basic structure to three-year full-time psychology degrees. (In Scotland, degrees usually last four years and it is best to consider the final two years as being similar to the final two years of a three-year degree in England and Wales.) Part-time degrees usually involve covering the material at a different rate taking up to six years, but it is best to examine individual part-time degree courses as some allow faster and slower part-time routes. It's worth noting that psychology degrees throughout the United Kingdom are fairly similar in their course content, because the British Psychological Society requires that certain areas must be covered if a degree is to be accredited.

Indicative degree structure:

Year 1: **Basic psychology, research methods and statistics, and key skills.**

Year 2: **Core areas including research methods and statistics.**

Year 3: **Empirical project in psychology (not a literature review) and options particular to a department.**

The core areas may extend into the third year and need to include the factors listed in Box 2:1.

Box 2:1 Core Areas of Degree Subject and Respective Content

Core area	Typical content (not exhaustive)
Cognitive Psychology	Perception, attention, learning, memory and language
Psychobiology	Basic neurochemistry, neurophysiology of nerve transmission, hormones and behaviour, biological bases of behaviour
Social Psychology	Attitudes, attributions, prejudice, social identification, conformity, obedience
Developmental Psychology	Perceptual, motor and cognitive development during infancy
Individual Differences	Genetic, environmental and cultural influences, psychological testing
Conceptual and Historical Issues	Scientific method, social and cultural construction of knowledge, history and philosophy of science
Research Methods and Statistics	Research design, quantitative methods including statistical tests

We've assumed that you're reading this book having already chosen somewhere to study, but if you haven't, check out the Appendix where we give advice on choosing the place that's right for you.

What if I Make the Wrong Choice?

It is possible to transfer between institutions should you feel that you've made the wrong choice, particularly from one degree offering GBR to another also offering GBR. However, if you want another university to take you, they will want to be confident that you can handle their degree. Obviously, that university would also have to have a place available, so the first thing to do is contact the admissions tutor and see if there is a possibility that you can move there. Remember that our advice in the Appendix about choosing a suitable course for you still applies even if you feel that you've made the wrong choice.

Before You Arrive at Your Chosen University

The most important thing to do before you start your degree is to ensure that, as far as possible, you have organised your life outside of study. You may have arranged accommodation on campus; if you do, ask to see your room as soon as possible to see what facilities it has (television aerial, Internet access and so on) as well as seeing how much storage and cupboard space is available. If you don't have accommodation on campus, make sure you have arranged your accommodation *before* you need to go in to university (normally for enrolment and induction). It is worth finding out if the university has an accommodation service, as they may be able to give you lists of properties that have received an inspection and have a landlord that hasn't (so far) caused problems for students. When considering if a property is suitable, do a test run of how long it takes to get to your place of study at the time that you would usually travel. For example, taking a bus in the afternoon is likely to take less time than in the rush hour when you are likely to be going in to the university. If you are in a rural area, you may find that the buses don't run at certain times of the day. It's also a good idea to find out if you will have some classes away from the main campus, as some universities in large cities have campuses that are spread over a very wide area.

If you have childcare responsibilities

If you need childcare support, it's a good idea to contact the university as soon as possible to see if there is a university nursery that would be suitable for you. Also, ask for a complete timetable for the whole year (ideally with deadlines for assessments) so that you can plan for half-term and so on.

Buying books

Some students are keen to obtain details of preparatory reading and it is worth finding out what books are required for the different subjects that you will be studying. However, it is a very good idea to try to speak to existing students first as they may tell you that they didn't find an 'essential' book all that essential! Also, in many departments there is an opportunity at the start of the academic year to purchase books from the students in the previous academic year, so you could save some money if you wait for that.

University libraries tend to have copies of core texts, but not enough for all students so for those core books you are probably going to have to buy a copy. Most universities have a bookshop on site that should stock all required books. However, the prices are normally the price printed on the book. To save money, you might want to check online booksellers as you can sometimes save large sums of money when buying a number of books. Our favourite is the most well known, Amazon (www.amazon.co.uk), but it is best to use a price comparison website like Kelkoo (www.kelkoo.co.uk) to see which is the cheapest for each of your books (remembering any postage and packing charges). We've already mentioned that students who have completed your year of the degree might sell their books at reduced rates, but check that those books are still required for a unit and that they are the most up-to-date editions. Some university student unions have secondhand bookstores where you can also save a lot of money. Finally, you could share a book with a friend, but we have found that doing so can lead to frustration since both students tend to want to use the book at the same time.

Enrolment and Induction

Usually in the week before the official start of term, universities have 'enrolment and induction' sessions. In enrolment, a member of the university may want to check your *original* certificates that were the basis for your acceptance on the degree. Photocopies will normally *not* be acceptable. In addition, you will need to complete various forms and procedures such as getting student ID, joining university societies and so on. Induction might be part of the same process and the content varies between different institutions. Some universities have minimal formal induction, but instead include induction in the first few weeks of a first-year course. Other institutions have more extensive induction sessions prior to the start of the teaching term. Whatever the precise arrangements, it is important to try to attend your induction as there will be useful information provided. It's best to get on top of this information at the start to avoid confusion later on. Induction also provides the first chance to meet the people who will be studying with you and who will, hopefully, become your friends.

The First Week

The first week of the degree can be chaotic, frustrating, confusing, overwhelming and frightening – and that's just for the lecturers! OK, it's not that bad, but it can be hectic because there is so much going on. There should be a fresher's week with lots of events (many involving alcohol, but also many that don't). There will be first lectures, perhaps with reading lists of books to obtain. There will be a timetable that may seem meaningless until you work it out and discover the coding used for rooms. There may be desperate searches for toilets, for edible food, for somewhere you can smoke, for somewhere you can have a break from it all. The important thing is to recognise that the first week is just that: you should quickly learn the location of the toilets, a good place to go and chat over a coffee and where your classes are taught. It's understood that students may find it difficult to find lecture theatres at first, so lecturers plan for late arrivals. Similarly, the first lecture is usually a gentle introduction that explains the structure of that part of the degree, so if you miss the start it is usually no great disaster.

The Second Week and Beyond

The second week is much calmer than the first and is when you can start settling into the pattern of your degree course. It is important to attend all the teaching situations that are available, that is, lectures, seminars and tutorials. As we've said, the first week or so is usually a general introduction to the content and procedures of each unit and if they are missed, you can catch up *with effort*. However, the biggest problem we've found is that students who miss sessions can become rapidly overwhelmed trying to catch up in addition to preparing for future teaching and reflecting on the teaching that they have attended. Think about what we said in the introduction about your life at university: you need to *organise*, *communicate* and *reflect*.

Do also make sure that you find out some of the mundane, but important, routine things that you need to know, such as:

- **Exactly when do classes start?**

- **The procedures for seeing staff (do I need to book to see staff in their offices?).**

- **Is there a particular member of the department I should see if I am having personal problems?**

- **Is there a particular member of the department I should see if I am having academic problems?**

- **How exactly do I submit work?**

- **What are the deadlines for my assessments?**

- **What is the policy and procedure for extensions?**

- **What allowance is made if I am seriously ill or suffer a death in the family?**

As the degree progresses you should ensure that you find out about the learning and personal support that is available for you. You can find support in a variety of places. In your psychology department you will get support from your tutors, other students and may even be offered extra sessions, for example, for statistics. Both the university and the student union will have services that offer advice and support on all aspects of student life, and you will find societies/support groups for women, ethnic and religious minorities and lesbian/gay/bi/transgendered individuals. Finally, you still have access to services that are available to the general public that can help you with general life problems, such as:

- **Citizens Advice Bureaux (www.nacab.org.uk)**

- **National Health Service (www.nhsdirect.nhs.uk)**

- **Samaritans (www.samaritans.org.uk).**

I've started late – help!

There are a variety of reasons why you might start a week or two late: illness, visa problems and accommodation problems. However, that isn't usually a big problem but you must see the course director to find out what you have missed and where you can obtain any handouts or lecture notes. So, make sure you see the course director or year tutor straight away otherwise you will find that your degree gets more complicated rather than simpler.

At the End of the First Year

The first year (first two years in Scotland) is essentially a foundation and you are usually only required to reach a pass standard so that you can progress into the second year. It's interesting to note that most universities don't include marks from the first year in their final degree classification. So, if you pass that first year you shouldn't have any worries. Having said that, if you have only just passed in one or more units, then you should consider why that happened. If you didn't do well on an examination because you were ill or had a temporary life crisis, then that's just 'one of those things'. If, however, your mark reflected fairly your understanding of an area, it is a very good idea to spend some time over the summer break working through the material, as most of those areas will be covered in more depth in the next two years of your degree.

If you fail a component or two of a unit, you may be allowed to redo those assessments during the summer. However, as soon as you fail an assessment, find out the regulations as you may discover that if you fail a certain number of assessments you will be required to leave without a chance of redoing those assessments.

I've failed and have to leave – my life is over ...

It can be devastating for students who have failed and are required to leave the degree. If you hadn't told the university about mitigating circumstances, you might want to submit a formal appeal, but you would need a good reason why you hadn't revealed those problems beforehand. If you don't have mitigating circumstances, you might feel that you've failed as a person and that your life is over. That's nonsense – ask Bill Gates, who didn't complete his university degree! Getting a degree is certainly not a guarantee of success and, similarly, not getting a degree is not a guarantee of failure. You need to ask yourself why you failed. It might not have been the right time in your life to do a degree. You might have enjoyed a little too much of the freedom of moving away from home and need to be more mature now. You might have belatedly realised that psychology is *not* for you and maybe you would succeed in another degree. You may simply have hated your university and would flourish at another. However, doing a degree may not be what's right for you and you might want to consider other options, depending on your skills and what *you* enjoy doing (rather than what other people – like parents or partners – think you *should* do).

At the End of the Second Year

At the end of your second year you should have a basic grounding in the key areas of psychology. You should have made your option choices and chosen a project area with those choices reflecting your interests or your intended career path – ideally both of those. It is also important to note that the second year of your degree *does* normally count towards the final degree, so failing one or two units can adversely affect your final degree classification.

At the End of the Third Year

Time for a celebratory drink and a party! Then, once the hangover has subsided, time to *continue* your career plan. In other words, it is not the time to *start* planning your career or *start* to submit job applications or applications for post-graduate study.

Although difficult, it really is worthwhile using your final semester to also make applications. One good reason is that after your graduation it is likely that many of your tutors will be away at conferences, writing books and journal articles, working at another department or possibly even having a holiday. As a result, reference requests received over that summer break can take a long time to get a response.

Getting the Most out of Your Degree

It's important to remember that lectures, seminars, practical work and tutorials are actually only a small part of the time you spend on your degree. The largest part of your degree is the time you spend in the library, on the Internet and in your 'office'. Your degree is what you make it. If you want a good degree, you need to take control of the process and use your time as effectively as possible. That still means having time for family and friends, since having good relationships with others is good for your mental health and should help you through stressful times. However, you need to discover the best way to manage yourself and others (Chapter 3), to understand what is involved in 'doing' psychology (Chapter 4), how to get the most out of out a variety of teaching situations (Chapter 5) so that you can do your best in your assessments (Chapter 6), how to use resources most effectively (Chapter 7), particularly for your psychology project (Chapter 8). Then you should be in a good position to do well after your degree (Chapter 9).

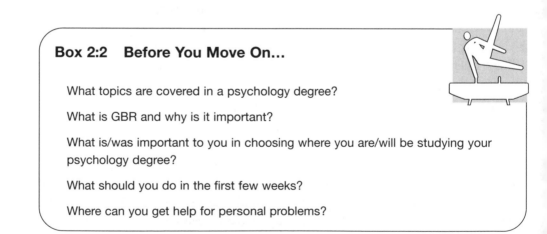

Box 2:2   Before You Move On...

What topics are covered in a psychology degree?

What is GBR and why is it important?

What is/was important to you in choosing where you are/will be studying your psychology degree?

What should you do in the first few weeks?

Where can you get help for personal problems?

3 Managing Yourself and Others

LEARNING OUTCOMES

1. To know how to write an effective email to a tutor.
2. To know how to get the most out of meetings with tutors.
3. To be aware of the etiquette of interacting with university staff.
4. To understand how to organise your work space and your time, and to manage your life outside of university more effectively.
5. To be aware of some of the key signs of depression and stress, and what to do about them.

Introduction

It is important that you consider how to deal with the wide variety of people that you will meet at university. It's also important that you think about how you are going to organise yourself. In this chapter we discuss some of those relationships and how you can get the most out of every interaction that you have.

Managing Your Relationships

Other people are human too! Like you, they have good days and they have bad days. In general, though, people respond well when they are treated well. If you can remember this, then your interactions with people at university are likely to be fruitful. In all your interactions you should remember our guidance to *organise*, *communicate* and *reflect* (OCR).

O

C

R

Box 3:1   OCR

For any interaction you should:

Organise: Ensure that you have established what you are trying to achieve *before* beginning your interaction, for example, have an agenda. Make sure you have identified all the relevant questions and documents that you need for the meeting.

Communicate: Ensure that you communicate efficiently, making use of your agenda and listening (and making notes) of what is said.

Reflect: Afterwards, you must reflect on what was said. Write a brief summary of the main outcomes from the meeting to help yourself with this. Did you forget any questions? Did you understand the answers? Are there any new questions that emerge from your reflection?

Your interactions with academic staff

You will encounter different sorts of academic staff during your degree. Most of them will probably be full-time permanent lecturing staff (called lecturers, senior lecturers and readers). Some of them may be professors who teach, whilst others may be responsible only for supervising their own research projects. You might interact with guest lecturers from other universities, or professionals such as clinical psychologists based elsewhere who do some teaching at your university. You may also find that post-graduate students studying for a PhD deliver some teaching (usually seminars).

The vast majority of academics have commitments in teaching, administration and research. The more prestigious the university, the likelier it is that the permanent academic staff will spend more of their time on research. Some of those academics may view teaching and undergraduates as a necessary evil, but you should find that most are enthusiastic about teaching as well as their research. However, this does mean that you need to remember that the staff are not just teaching you, but are busy with other things as well. Therefore, you need to help them to help you, which requires using that OCR approach yet again.

Remember that staff can deal with your queries in a variety of ways. For example, brief queries can usually be addressed by email. Longer questions (or questions requiring longer answers) may be better addressed in their tutorial hours and perhaps during their teaching slots (for example, seminars). Outside of term time you can still use email, but remember that staff also have vacations, attend conferences or may work with collaborators at other psychology departments anywhere in the world.

Before contacting staff, do *please* make sure that you have looked for the answer to the question in any course materials that you have been given. In our department, we provide a one-page sheet of frequently asked questions (FAQ) and we're amazed how often we *still* get asked those same questions. If your department doesn't have something like that, why not ask your tutors if you could have one. Also make sure that the question is an *appropriate* one for a tutor; if you have forgotten the procedure on how to hand in work, for example, then it is probably better to contact a member of the administrative staff rather than one of your tutors.

You may have noticed that we haven't mentioned using the telephone to contact staff. You may come across one or two academics who aren't keen on using email and may prefer to use the telephone, but the majority prefer *not* to use the telephone and it's worth thinking about why that might be. If you ring one of your lecturers, they are either in their office or they are not. If they are in their office, it is unlikely that they are gazing out of the window feeling lonely (though not impossible). Generally, when an academic is in their office they are reading something (normally quite complicated), marking something, writing or doing something else, well, academic. On the other hand, they may be in a meeting with undergraduate students, research students, colleagues or visitors. In none of those situations is it convenient to receive a telephone call. If they do take a call, they are unlikely to give the issue their full attention. In fact, most calls we do receive are pretty straightforward and are actually answered in our course guide or unit guide, or are too complicated to deal with on the telephone. If they are too complicated, we ask the student to send a detailed email so that we can deal with the issue and then send a detailed reply or ask the student to book an appropriate amount of time for a tutorial.

However, there is the other outcome: there is no reply, so the student leaves a message. The first problem here is that most of us hate talking to answerphones, become embarrassed and nervous and very rarely leave 'good' messages. We sometimes receive messages that go something like 'Oh, er, I was, er, hoping to speak to you. I guess you're not there. So I can't speak to you. Well, I was hoping to speak, er, discuss this problem that I had, well it's still a bit of a problem, but I wondered if, if you could help me with it so can you call me on' and then give their telephone number as fast as they possibly can and sometimes it's even inaudible. Even if the telephone number is audible, the academic has a problem; they know *absolutely nothing* about the problem. The problem could actually be very simple or it could be incredibly complicated, so if they ring the student back the call could take seconds or maybe an hour. That uncertainty makes it impossible to judge whether the few minutes before the lecturer has to leave for the next meeting are going to be sufficient to deal with that issue. The other problem is that calling students (somewhat perversely since most now use mobile phones) is hit and miss. All lecturers have played 'telephone tennis', where we leave messages for students and keep on missing the return call, so we call back leave a message and so on. So, we hope you can see that while the telephone is a marvellous invention, it normally isn't the best way to contact academics.

We believe that emails are one of the most effective ways of communicating with staff, and it's worth considering why that *is* the case. For students, one of the big advantages is that you don't have to worry too much about dealing with someone you might find intimidating. If some of your tutors are famous psychologists, it can be very scary asking them questions and you can get nervous, but if you send an email you can spend time putting together your question and can provide relevant background information that you would be too nervous to remember face-to-face. You can even ask a friend to check what you've written if you are worried. An added convenience is that you can write an email at any time that is convenient for you – day or night. Email is not only convenient for the student, it's also convenient for the staff as it can be dealt with at a convenient time and it's not a problem to break off an email to go to teach and then resume that email when you return. In essence, it gives both students and staff *control* over their lives. Finally, it's worth noting that emails are easier to read than handwritten notes and it's far easier to reply to them! You should always consider the information that you include in an email to someone.

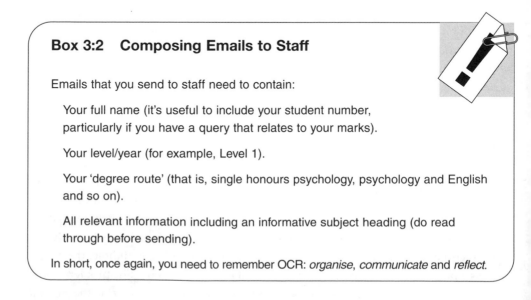

Box 3:2   Composing Emails to Staff

Emails that you send to staff need to contain:

Your full name (it's useful to include your student number, particularly if you have a query that relates to your marks).

Your level/year (for example, Level 1).

Your 'degree route' (that is, single honours psychology, psychology and English and so on).

All relevant information including an informative subject heading (do read through before sending).

In short, once again, you need to remember OCR: *organise, communicate* and *reflect.*

You might think this is obvious, but it's surprising how many emails we receive that are along the lines of:

From: fluffybunny696@hotmail.com
Subject: [none]
I am really enjoying your class. I frgot to write down that reference that you mentioned.
Can you tell me what it was!

Er, what?! We teach three levels of undergraduate teaching and a post-graduate course. Reading this, we don't know which level/year this student is (or even their name) and what unit or even the week to which 'fluffybunny696' is referring. Of course, the student knew this information but forgot that the reader would not. Make sure you don't make this mistake! Also, it isn't a good idea to use 'funny' email addresses as it's fun for friends, but it doesn't exactly give you credibility, which can be a problem when you are asking for references. Funny email addresses also mean that your identity isn't immediately clear when you write to someone or could even be dismissed as spam.

Box 3:3   Sending Emails

Write an email as you normally would, asking the question in the text example or something similar.

Then ask yourself if you have supplied all the information listed in the checklist and all the information that a lecturer might need to answer.

Finally, think about how OCR might help you use email more effectively.

However, we're not suggesting that all communication should be in the form of emails. If you want a specific answer, then emails are good. For example, asking for an exact reference, seeking advice on suitable journals for an essay or asking a specific question about something said in a lecture are all suitable questions for emails. But if what you really need is a discussion, then email is too limited. When you need to discuss an issue, such as a variety of options available to you if you're having problems or discussing ideas for a final year project or even trying to completely understand a theory that was presented in a lecture, then a face-to-face meeting is generally better.

Your meetings with academic staff

Organise
When attending a meeting with a tutor, *you* must have an agenda. What that means is that you need to work out what you want to achieve from the meeting and how you can best do that. This does not mean that you should 'take charge' of the meeting, but rather that you facilitate the tutor to help you. It is always worth considering whether you should

provid any information before the meeting. However, do be realistic and don't email a ten-page document the evening before a meeting and expect the tutor to have read it!

Communicate

For the meeting itself, do ensure that you take along pen and paper to take notes. Also, do make sure that you use them! We are amazed at how often students come to ask us about a detailed technical matter and sit in front of us listening, but not taking any notes whatsoever. You need to take notes so that you can check that you have understood that issue.

Reflect

You should plan some dedicated time after the meeting so you can think about what *you* said and what the *tutor* said. Writing a brief summary of the meeting is useful. You may want to make a note of things you said and did that seemed to provoke a positive response and things you spoke or did that received a more negative response. It is likely that the more prepared you were on a topic, the more positive a response you received. Also, you may realise that you forgot to ask a question, or a further question might have subsequently arisen, and you should either book another meeting or consider emailing if it is suitable for your follow-up.

Finally, *please* make sure that you're on time. If you have booked a 20-minute slot with a tutor, it is likely that they have booked in someone else after you, so if you are 15 minutes late you will have lost *your* time and not the time of the person who is after you. (Note also that you will have wasted the time of the tutor.) Also, it is quite simply rude to turn up late for a meeting, so if you are unavoidably delayed do try to contact that person by telephone so that they are informed and they might even be able to delay the end of your meeting. After all, how would *you* want to be treated?

Your interactions with office staff

Much of what we've said above about dealing with academic staff applies to office staff also. By 'office staff' we mean people who work in the accommodation office, fees office, finance office and your department or faculty administrative staff. In particular, you may have several people who are dedicated course administrators for the psychology degree(s). Course administrators are the people who deal with administrative matters relating to the degree, for example, submission and return of coursework, return of student marks, despatch of various official letters and providing guidance on non-academic matters. These people are your friends – or should be! They are people who can offer advice and generally help you, but are unlikely to put themselves out for you if you are rude.

One difficult situation for office staff is working on a counter dealing with student queries, as these interactions can be tiring. It can be like working at an airport check-in desk and could be stressful for both them and you. If things have gone wrong, it's always best to avoid complaining aggressively to the person in front of you if you want to achieve the best results. You need to focus on what you want to achieve and be as polite and friendly as possible (OCR again!). Remember, when dealing with organisations like universities or airlines, the person who has let you down (for example, by cancelling a flight) is almost never the poor person who has to deal with the angry victims of that failure.

Your interactions with technical and library staff

Technical staff and library staff are highly skilled individuals who usually have a degree (or two) and can pass on hints and tricks to help you with your degree. For example, laboratory staff should know how to get equipment to work with the minimum of fuss and the library staff can help you use a variety of databases. If you have a psychology 'subject librarian', they can often give you a great deal of detailed help using the psychology resources of the library. Again, remember to always be polite. Once again, OCR is important. You should ensure that you know exactly what you want to do (as far as possible) and it is often worth pre-booking if you want to explore possibilities. You need to communicate effectively, ensuring that they understand your requirements (remember that they may not be familiar with the requirements of your psychology degree). Always ensure that you reflect on what was said afterwards as you may realise that technical terms were used and you may not be sure that you have understood those terms correctly.

Won't people think I'm stupid if I keep checking up on things?

Not at all. When you follow up a discussion by checking the meaning of a technical term, you are demonstrating that you want to make use of that discussion. You are demonstrating that you don't want to waste either your time or the time of the person with whom you were talking. If anything, people are likely to think that you are careful and diligent, not stupid.

Your interactions with your fellow students

In the previous chapter, we have already mentioned how you will meet a lot of new people when you begin your degree. In addition to the intrinsic value in friendships, it's important to note the value of student friends in helping you to do well in your degree, and hopefully you can do the same for them – it's not a competition, after all!

You may even want to pair up with a 'study buddy', to use an ugly American phrase. A study buddy is someone who is taking the same classes as you (essentially lectures, seminars and practicals) who undertakes to collect handouts when you can't attend due to illness. In addition, they discuss work with you outside classes and share discoveries (for example, another good library nearby, a good bookshop, a lecture series being held nearby, useful Internet sites, relevant television programmes), good practices (for example, ways of taking notes) and finding out if your confusion over instructions is shared so that you feel more comfortable asking the relevant person for clarification. And you do the same for them. However, take very great care if you work together on written work as it is easy to collude rather than collaborate; see Chapter 6 'Assessments' for further guidance.

In general you should 'do unto others as you would have them do unto you'. That simply means that you don't disrupt others by talking in the library, computer rooms or classes. In particular, don't arrive late for classes and always turn off your mobile phone – the most frequent complaint we receive from students about their fellow students!

Being friendly with your fellow students brings many advantages. However, it's worth highlighting a potential danger – plagiarism. Lending coursework to fellow students is a generous but risky thing to do. We have dealt with a number of cases where one student has lent completed coursework to another student who, due to lack of time, copied large chunks of that material. *Both* students were subsequently charged with academic misconduct, which is very distressing and could result in serious penalties even for the person who innocently lent their work, particularly if the other person won't accept the blame. (We say more about plagiarism – what it is and how to avoid it – in Chapter 6.)

I've had enough of being nice – I want to complain!

Complaining is fine and it's important to do so when things go wrong. Your department should have various quality control mechanisms such as student feedback being collected at the end of units, regular meetings of staff with student representatives and clear mechanisms for you to make a complaint. However, bear in mind what we said earlier – your problem is unlikely to have been caused by the person you deal with, so lay off them! If you do need to complain, make sure you use our OCR method. You should identify what it is you want to achieve by your complaint and how you can best make that happen.

Managing Yourself

It's easy to think only about managing others, or rather, managing your interactions with others. However, the most important person you need to manage is yourself.

You may have already seen books with titles like 'Top ten tips for good time management' or at school been taught how to use various techniques for studying. However, we aren't going to do that here. Instead, we think it's most important for *you* to decide what works best for *you*. In particular, you need to be realistic about what you can and can't achieve in a given time. In a way, it's very similar to effective weight loss. Some people can go out running long distances every day. Some people can just as happily eat lovely salads as eat burger and chips. But most of us find it hard to stick to rigorous exercise regimes and are often tempted by fast food. So most of us have to think hard about how we keep our weight as we want it.

You may be surprised by the emphasis we are placing on being organised. Doesn't success depend on how intelligent you are? It's certainly true that getting a first-class rather than a third-class degree requires intelligence, but what really makes the difference between success and failure seems to be dependent on other factors too. Indeed, recent research (Robbins *et al.*, 2004) suggests that performance and whether or not students continue their studies is predicted by a student's self-belief, motivation and having the tools to manage academic demands.

Here's the full reference for that journal article:

Robbins, S.B., Lauver, K., Le, H., Davis, D. and Langley, R. (2004). Do psychosocial and study skill factors predict college outcomes? A meta-analysis. *Psychological Bulletin, 130*, 261–88.

Being organised means that you can make the most of your abilities.

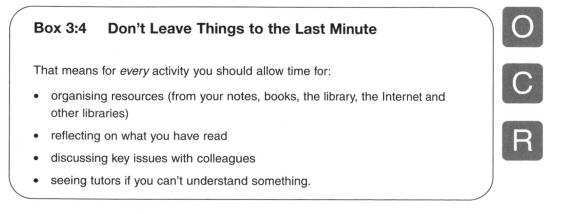

Box 3:4   Don't Leave Things to the Last Minute

That means for *every* activity you should allow time for:

- organising resources (from your notes, books, the library, the Internet and other libraries)
- reflecting on what you have read
- discussing key issues with colleagues
- seeing tutors if you can't understand something.

In Chapter 5 we discuss how to make the most of various 'Teaching Situations', but for now we just want to point out that you should not 'rob Peter to pay Paul' by skipping on:

- **reading ahead of classes**

- **attending lectures and seminars**

- **doing the exercises set in seminars.**

That might seem obvious, but remember that when your tutors set you tasks it is because they believe the tasks should help you, not because they think you should keep yourself occupied.

Creating an 'office'

We aren't suggesting that you go mad on DIY, but we do think it's a good idea if you have some place that you can think of as your office. If you're very lucky, you may have a spare room, but more usually it will be the corner of a room. It could even be a quiet spot in your university or local library. All that you need to do is ensure that the resources you will need are available there, that it has good lighting and is comfortable (that is, a good chair and neither too hot nor too cold). Most important, especially if you have children or a partner living with you, is to try to have 'office hours'. Just like your tutors have time set aside to see you on a one-to-one basis, you should designate time to work by yourself without interruptions. The time and frequency of those office hours will be up to you. You may find that you work best if you get up very early (perhaps before everyone else) or you may find that you work better when everyone else has gone to bed.

Computer resources

One of the things that can make a difference to your student experience is whether or not you have good access to computer resources. Your university *should* give you access to a large number of computers, but you may find that they can be heavily used at certain times. Those busy times are likely to be lunchtime most days, as well as the time when final year projects are due to be handed in.

Is it worth buying a computer?

Well, investing in your own computer is certainly not going to be a disadvantage, but it's a similar question to 'Is it worth buying all the recommended texts?'. The main disadvantages are likely to be the cost and the space required for one. The advantages are that you can work on your assessments (essays, practical reports and projects), practise using software (for example, SPSS) and use your library's electronic resources (usually with appropriate passwords) if you are connected to the Internet.

If you think buying a computer is a worthwhile purchase *for you*, consider the options detailed below.

Laptop vs. desktop PC

Laptops are small and portable, but that makes them easier to steal and you can be a tempting target for muggers if you are carrying a laptop case in the street or on public transport. Laptop components are harder to upgrade as everything is packed in tightly and they don't tend to last as long if they are being carried around. PCs are cheaper and have better screens, but tend to be large (especially the monitor) and space is usually in demand in most households in Britain.

Microsoft vs. Mac PC

Mac computers are aesthetically more attractive, easier to use and more fun than normal PCs that run Microsoft software. Unfortunately, they are now very much the minority among personal computers, so unless your university has lots of them you may find it a lot harder to find software (for example, SPSS from your university) and support (for example, friends who also use Macs).

New vs. old

Because computers are so common, even at home, but are replaced often, you may be offered an old PC. Is it worth buying or using an old PC? It may be the best decision for you, but do be wary. You might find that your old computer cannot use the latest software, won't enable you to plug in hardware such as memory sticks or even use a new printer. Try to get advice from an experienced computer user, but remember that salespeople will usually try to sell you things, hence the name!

What is essential?

Any PC you want to use must have a CD drive so that you can install software. You also really do need a printer (and there are very cheap new ones available, but replacement cartridges can be very expensive so check out ink refill kits too). It's also very useful to have an Internet connection, even if it's a relatively slow one that costs something like a penny a minute. In fact, one advantage of university-owned student accommodation is that, increasingly, high-speed Internet access is being made available in each student room.

What software will I be using in the degree?

During your degree you will almost certainly use some specialised psychology software, either for teaching purposes (for example, the British Psychological Society Statistics CD-ROM) or for collecting data (for example, PsychLab). However, you will also use a variety of standard packages and being able to use them are key skills for your CV. For example, you will need to use a word processing package (for example, MS Word), a web browser (for example, MS Internet Explorer) and an email package (for example, Pegasus mail or MS Outlook). In addition, you will use a statistics programme such as SPSS or maybe Minitab. If you buy a computer, you may find some of these packages included in the price. If they aren't you should find out if your university can supply these for you (usually on a CD) at a massively reduced cost. For example, our university supplies the student version of SPSS on CD for free, whereas it sells for over £50 on the Internet!

If you have your own computer, you *must* have anti-virus software (with updated virus definitions) and if you use the Internet from home, make sure you have a firewall. You can find out information about both anti-virus software and firewalls on the Internet – just use www.google.com or download examples from www.tucows.com.

Why is it so important to back up files?

What's the classic excuse for not handing in work at school? The dog ate my homework. (Actually, one of us once had in fact a teacher who was embarrassed to admit to our class that her dog had in fact eaten our homework!) The classic excuse at university is that a computer 'ate' the assessment. Most of the time this is probably true, but generally it is excluded as a legitimate reason for work being submitted late as it's almost impossible to verify. In fact, students do not have a good reason for that problem, as you should always back up files. In short, always back up on to a floppy disk, a CD or a removable device such as a memory stick. Alternatively, why not email your work to your Internet email account to keep it safe.

Organising your notes

This might seem really obvious, but you need to make sure that you're organised from the moment you start your degree. When you arrive, you may be given large amounts of handouts, some of which you need to keep, some that can be thrown away and some that you actually must read, such as your course guide. When you get your timetable, you will usually see that you are doing three or four units each semester. You should consider using one folder for each unit and keep handouts and notes in the same place. This means you do not have to carry all your material around with you, but that you can just take out the materials you actually intend to use that day.

Attend all the lectures and ensure that you have all handouts – and read them when you get them! One of us had lectures on a Saturday. Yes, Saturday. Funnily enough, not many of those lectures were attended, but handouts were obtained from a friendly fellow student who didn't stay out so late on Friday night/Saturday morning. That seemed like a cunning plan to avoid those lectures, but the funny thing is that lecture notes that make perfect sense when you hear the lecture suddenly seem incomprehensible when viewed 'cold'. What's worse is that you discover that problem only when you start revising. We've seen this problem ourselves when we get student feedback, as students who complain about the quality of lecture handouts always seem to be the ones that we don't recognise!

Getting the Balance Right

Studying for a degree takes at least three years and can be longer if you study in Scotland where degrees last four years and even longer if you study part-time. That's a long time and it is essential to ensure that you get the balance right between study and the other things in your life. Doing a degree involves hard work, but should also be a lot of fun as you will meet new people and have new experiences (hopefully all legal). Do remember that your personal relationships (especially if you have children or other dependants) are important. You might find it useful to create a timetable with allocations for non-university activities.

Sometimes students find that studying at university can become too much and feel that they cannot cope. This can sometimes be a manifestation of depression and/or anxiety and isn't that unusual so if that happens to you, do not be frightened to talk to one of your tutors so that they can direct you to the most appropriate source of advice. But there are some general guidelines of what to look for, in yourself and others, to spot someone who is at risk.

Spotting depression

Depression is usually diagnosed using what are called 'criteria lists' to enable reliable diagnosis. You may already be familiar with the Beck Depression Inventory and DSM-IV (Diagnostic and Statistical Manual of Mental Disorders). The material below is adapted from the NHS Direct website (www.nhsdirect.nhs.uk), which provides information about a number of mental health issues. If you use that website, do be careful of matching symptoms to various illnesses – most headaches are *not* brain tumours!

You should seek help if over the last two weeks, five of the following features have been present, of which one or more should be depressed mood most of the day, nearly every day, or loss of interest or pleasure in almost all activities most of the day, nearly every day. And the remaining (the total to make at least five) from any of the following:

- **Significant weight loss or gain (more than 5 per cent change in one month) or an increase or decrease in appetite nearly every day.**

- **Insomnia or sleeping too much nearly every day.**

- **Psychomotor agitation or retardation nearly every day (observable by others, not merely subjective feelings of restlessness or being slowed down).**

- **Fatigue or loss of energy nearly every day.**

- **Feelings of worthlessness or excessive or inappropriate guilt (which may be delusional) nearly every day (not merely self reproach about being sick).**

- **Diminished ability to think or concentrate, or indecisiveness, nearly every day (either by subjective account or observation of others).**

- **Recurrent thoughts of death (not just fear of dying).**

- **Recurrent suicidal ideation without a specific plan or a suicide attempt or a specific plan for committing suicide.**

- **The symptoms cause clinically significant distress or impairment in occupational or other important areas of functioning.**

Spotting anxiety

Anxiety can be a crippling problem, but sufferers often avoid seeking help. Sometimes the anxiety can be caused by specific events such as exam anxiety or may be a response to specific things such as phobias. However, there is a type of anxiety called generalised anxiety disorder (GAD) where sufferers cannot seem to shake off their worries, even though they usually realize that their anxiety is more severe than the situation warrants. Anxiety may involve an exaggerated startle response, lack of concentration, irritability, trouble falling or staying asleep, narrowing of attention span, reduced mental efficiency, and a tendency for the mind to 'go blank'.

In addition to these mental disturbances, there are physical disturbances that include:

- **muscle tension and sometimes teeth-grinding**

- **trembling, particularly of hands**

- **restlessness**

- **sweating, flushing**

- **dry mouth**

- **lightheadedness**

- **nausea, diarrhoea, abdominal colic, frequent urination**

- **a 'lump in the throat'**

- **a feeling of tightness in the chest, breathlessness, palpitations, rapid pulse**

- **weakness, fatigue**

- **headache**

- **loss of appetite.**

If you think you are suffering from anxiety, you really should seek help as it's unlikely to just go away. It's also important to exclude a physical problem so it would be wise to see your GP first.

Important

If you are suffering from depression and/or anxiety, it is unlikely that your lecturers will be able to help you directly by offering you counselling themselves (it's unlikely that they are chartered clinical psychologists or chartered counselling psychologists). Instead, you should first see your GP to ensure that there is not a physical reason for your problems (such as thyroid problems for anxiety). Then, you should seek counselling and/or drug treatments through your GP or you may prefer to use your university counselling service.

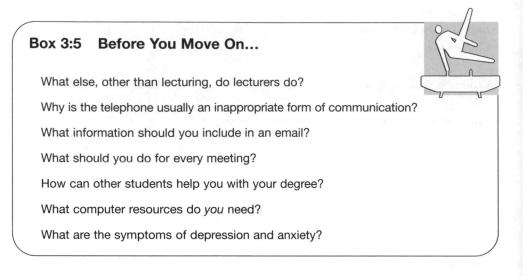

Box 3:5   Before You Move On...

What else, other than lecturing, do lecturers do?

Why is the telephone usually an inappropriate form of communication?

What information should you include in an email?

What should you do for every meeting?

How can other students help you with your degree?

What computer resources do *you* need?

What are the symptoms of depression and anxiety?

4 Doing Psychology

LEARNING OUTCOMES

1. To understand why the scientific method is important for the student of psychology.
2. To be aware of the distinction between quantitative and qualitative methods.
3. To understand some of the basic ideas behind experiments and observational studies.
4. To be aware of the distinction between descriptive statistics and inferential statistics.
5. To be able to use a short guide to picking the appropriate statistical test.
6. To know how to use statistical output and understand what that output tells you about your study.

Introduction

In 1973, the eminent physicist Professor Jacob Brownowski presented a landmark documentary series on the BBC called *The Ascent of Man*. In an episode called 'Knowledge or Certainty', Brownowski considered the limits to knowledge and finished with a piece to camera in the Nazi concentration camp at Auschwitz. Brownowski said:

> It is said that science will dehumanise people and turn them into numbers. That is false: tragically false. Look for yourself. This is the concentration camp and crematorium at Auschwitz. *This* is where people were turned into numbers. Into this pond were flushed the ashes of some four million people. And that was not done by gas. It was done by arrogance. It was done by dogma. It was done by ignorance. When people believe that they have absolute knowledge, with no test in reality, this is how they behave. This is what men do when they aspire to the knowledge of gods. ... Science is a very human

form of knowledge. We are always at the brink of the known; we always feel forward for what is to be hoped. Every judgment in science stands on the edge of error, and is personal. Science is a tribute to what we can know, *although* we are fallible. In the end, the words were said by Oliver Cromwell, 'I beseech you, in the bowels of Christ. Think it possible you may be mistaken.'

You may be surprised that an expert in physics is talking about science being very human and judgments in science being personal. You may have thought that science was about *proving* things to be true or false. You may expect psychology to *prove*, for example, that men are more intelligent than women (or vice versa). Unfortunately, that's not what psychology, or indeed any science, actually does. Sciences attempt to develop theories that explain phenomena, and to put those theories to rigorous empirical test. For you to do this, you must use OCR.

Box 4:1 Using OCR

Doing psychology successfully demands that you prepare and organise your psychological practical work with a great deal of care and attention. If you fail to do this, then you are likely to run into problems that you can't solve. For example, it's no good realising that an experimental task is too difficult for your participants or that you've forgotten to run a control group *after* you have run the experiment. You need to plan your practical work with great thoroughness, and wherever possible undertake pilot studies since it's difficult to think of everything that might go wrong ahead of actually conducting the study. It also demands the ability to communicate effectively in two respects. First, you need to communicate your intentions to your participants effectively. It's no good, for example, if questions on a questionnaire you have designed are ambiguous. Second, you need to be able to communicate your findings effectively (we give advice and guidance on this in Chapters 6 and 7). And, of course, you need to reflect on what you are trying to achieve and to reflect on past mistakes you have made in your practical work to ensure that you don't make them again.

The Scientific Method

It is important to have a basic understanding of what is meant by the scientific method, although you should be aware that there are many controversial questions about how science works.

In essence science works by testing theories. It does this by *deducing* predictions from a theory and then testing to see whether or not the prediction turns out to be true or false.

(If the idea of deducing a prediction from a theory is not familiar to you, it is explained below.) If the test shows that the prediction is true, that's good news for the theory as it has received some confirmation. But if the prediction turns out to be false, then that's bad news for the theory, and it will either have to be rejected or amended. In psychology, we usually call such predictions 'hypotheses'. This is called the 'hypothetico-deductive method'.

Here's an example from psychology. In the 1950s, the American psychologist Tolman was interested in testing a theory about animal learning that said that animals learn only when they are rewarded. For instance, if hungry rats are placed in a maze they will gradually find their way out. If you reward the rats with food each time they find their way through the maze, then they get better and better at finding their way through as measured by a decreasing number of wrong turns, for example. Let's call this condition 1 – where hungry rats are rewarded. Rats that are hungry but are never rewarded do not improve their performance. Let's call this condition 2 – where hungry rats are never rewarded. Tolman wondered whether the unrewarded rats might nonetheless be learning about the fastest way to get through the maze, but not demonstrating their learning because they had no motive for doing so. So, he introduced a third condition – where a group of hungry rats were treated as in condition 2 for the first ten days of the experiment, but then rewarded on the eleventh day. He predicted that if they were learning, then their performance on getting through the maze should dramatically improve on the twelfth day. His prediction was confirmed. The rats' performance did dramatically improve on the twelfth day in condition 3. This provides confirmation for his idea that rats learn even when not rewarded.

Deduction

The basic idea behind the hypothetico-deductive method is that a prediction is *deduced* from a theory and then subjected to test. To understand what is going on you need to have a basic understanding of deductively valid argument. This sounds complicated, but it's really very straightforward. A deductively valid argument is one where *if* its premises are true, then its conclusion *must* be true (note the *if*). Here's an example:

Premise 1:   The person who is the Vice-Chancellor of LSBU has an IQ of over 150.
Premise 2:   If a person has an IQ of over 150, then they will have an income of more than £200,000 per year.
Conclusion: The person who is Vice-Chancellor of LSBU has an income of over £200,000 per year.

Now, we do *not* know if premise 1 is true. We also do *not* know if premise 2 is true. We do *not* know if the conclusion is true. But what we *do know for certain* is that *if* the premises are true, then the conclusion *must* be true.

If you do not see this, think of it as illustrated in Box 4:2.

Box 4:2 If the Premises are True, then the Conclusion Must be True

As we know, a deductively valid argument is one in which the truth of the premises guarantees the truth of the conclusion. Now, what this means is that we will not be able to think up a case where the premises are true and the conclusion is false without contradiction. (A contradiction is where you hold one proposition to be both true and false at the same time.)

First, we are going to imagine an example where the premises are true. Suppose we have two lists – list A and list B. On list A are the names of all the people with IQs of over 150. On list B are the names of all the people with incomes of more than £200,000 per annum. Premise 1 says that the V-C of LSBU has an IQ of over 150. So we can make this true if we imagine the list to be like this:

```
Richard Branson
Tony Blair
Jeffrey Weeks
S-G Erikson
V-C of LSBU
…
…
…
List A: IQ > 150
```

NB: > means 'greater than'

Premise 2 says that if we find that a person is on list A, we will also find them on list B. So premise 2 is true when all the names on list A are also on list B. The two lists below, therefore, illustrate what has to be the case for premise 1 to be true.

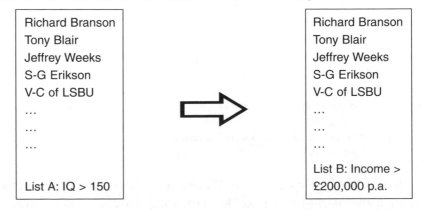

You can think of the arrow as a transfer mechanism that takes names from list A and puts them on list B and thus ensures the premise is true.

(Continued)

Box 4:2   (Continued)

Second, we have to illustrate the falsity of the conclusion. Remember – our task was to think up a case where the premises are true and the conclusion is false.

Well, if the conclusion is false, then the V-C of LSBU should not be on list B. So, we illustrate the falsity of the conclusion by removing the V-C of LSBU from list B so that it now looks like this:

Richard Branson
Tony Blair
Jeffrey Weeks
S-G Erikson
...
...
...

List B: Income > £200,000 p.a.

But now we have made the conclusion false, we've also made premise 2 false. You can see this by comparing this version of list B with the version (on the left) that made premise 2 true. Premise 2 is *not* true if the V-C of LSBU is not on list B!

Collecting psychological data

Once you have your prediction or hypothesis you need to design a study to test it. A major way in which psychologists study the human mind and behaviour is by carrying out controlled laboratory experiments. Consider the Tolman example again. He was studying learning in rats and he investigated this experimentally. So, he had to find a way to decide whether a rat has learned, and to find a way of measuring how much it has learned. He has to find a way to *operationalise* the idea of learning in rats. He did this by counting the number of wrong turns a rat makes in a maze. Psychologists refer to what a psychologist measures as a 'dependent variable' (or DV). It is called 'dependent' because the psychologist will want to try to show that change in this variable is or is not due (is or is not dependent on) some other variable that the psychologist can manipulate or vary between groups in the experiment. This latter variable is known as the 'independent variable' (or IV). In Tolman's case he manipulates how rats are rewarded and varies this between three groups of rats. As we described earlier, one group is rewarded on each day from day one, a second group are not rewarded at all, and a third group are rewarded for the first time on the tenth day of the experiment. He predicted that if rats are learning without reward, then the rats that are rewarded on the tenth day should show an immediate and dramatic increase in their performance (as measured by wrong turns). If, however, rats do not learn unless rewarded, then there should be no significant increase in performance. Tolman's results suggested that rats do learn even when not rewarded. Indeed, you should be able to see that it is difficult to explain why the rats in the third group should behave as they did on the eleventh day if they had not been learning all along.

You may wonder if experiments can be effectively carried out on people as well as on rats – well, they can!

Box 4:3   The False Belief Test

Here is a simple example of a very famous experiment on children. This experiment was reported in 1983 by the psychologists Joseph Perner and Hans Wimmer. They were interested in the age at which children understand the idea that other people behave in accordance with their beliefs about the world and not on the basis of the way the world actually is. We do, of course, try to get our beliefs to be in accord with the way the world is, but we don't always succeed – we sometimes form false beliefs. Understanding this is often a key to understanding other people's behaviour. So, you can understand why I missed the start of the film I wanted to go to see if you realize that I had a false belief about when the film was due to begin. You realise, perhaps, that I believed the film started at 8.00 p.m. and so I didn't leave the house until 7.30 p.m., which didn't give me enough time to get to the cinema for the actual start which was 7.45 p.m.

Perner and Wimmer wanted to find out at what age children could use the idea that another person has a false belief to explain the other's behaviour. They devised a cunning experiment. They told children a story about two characters: Sally and Anne. In the story, Sally has a chocolate and she wants to keep it to eat later, so she places it in a basket. She then goes out to play. Anne decides to play a trick on Sally and she moves the chocolate from the basket to a box while Sally is out playing. Then Sally returns and wants to eat her chocolate. Children are now asked the crucial question: 'Where will Sally look for her chocolate?' Now Sally, of course, believes that her chocolate is in the basket, since that's where she put it, and she wasn't there when Anne moved it. What Perner and Wimmer found was that children under the age of four say that Sally will look for her chocolate in the box! But children older than four say that she will look for it in the basket. The former age group do not appear to understand that people act on the basis of their beliefs (even if false) and not on the basis of how the world actually is. This is known as the 'false belief test' and has been used widely in developmental psychology in all sorts of ways, including trying to understand childhood autism.

You might like to try to identify the DV and the IV in this experiment.

Wimmer, H. and Perner, J. (1983). Beliefs about beliefs: Representation and constraining function of wrong beliefs in young children's understanding of deception. *Cognition*, 13, 103–128.

Carrying out experiments is a major way of collecting data to test a theory. But it is not the only way. Another major way of collecting data is by means of careful observation. (Other research methods that you should encounter in your degree are interviews and questionnaires, but discussing them is beyond the scope of this chapter.) In their simplest forms, they each have a main advantage and disadvantage (see Box 4:4).

Box 4:4   Research Method Advantages and Disadvantages

Research method	Advantage	Disadvantage
Observation	Naturalistic	Poor control
Experiment	Good control	Non-naturalistic

These differences are illuminating. Naturalism is important in psychology. We are really interested in natural human behaviour. If someone asked you how memory works, they want to know how memory works in normal life, not how it works on weird tasks. However, when we have naturalism we tend to have poor control of the situation, so we can't study *exactly* what we want to. For example, we might be interested in the ways in which people avoid bumping into each other (there are gender differences in whether people turn towards or away from the other person to avoid colliding). That is perfectly suited for simple observation, but if we wanted to test specific hypotheses, such as what happens when a tall woman avoids a collision with a short man who is carrying something, then we might have to wait a long time for that situation to occur naturally. We have to balance out control and naturalism in such cases and use our critical thinking to decide which is most important.

However, it is important to note that for each study we might choose between observation or experiment, but that when we try to understand something like human memory, we don't expect that one study will answer all our questions! It is essential to remember that researchers work to build up a body of knowledge and use a variety of different techniques. So, you might start off with an experiment, then carry out an observational study and then perform another experiment.

Quantitative/Qualitative Distinction

When you study psychology, you should be introduced to two different ways of doing psychology that can be characterised as quantitative and qualitative. In practice, those approaches are not mutually exclusive and it's more a case of the degree to which an approach is thought of as more quantitative or more qualitative. The distinction relates to the treatment of data, rather than methods as such. Some psychologists get very animated about demonstrating which of these is 'best', but more sensible psychologists consider these two approaches to be complementary. Choosing between the two reflects the particular question being addressed or the particular skills and background of a researcher.

In Box 4:5 we highlight the key characteristics of the two approaches.

Box 4:5   Key Characteristics of Qualitative and Quantitative Approaches

Qualitative	Quantitative
Words as the unit of analysis	*Numbers* as the unit of analysis
Visible analytic *description*	Visible *analysis*
Small-scale studies	*Large-scale* studies
Holistic perspective	*Specific* focus
Researcher *involvement*	Researcher *detachment*
Emergent research design	*Predetermined* research design

Ethics

Psychologists, including students of psychology, must adhere to ethical principles in their empirical work. That means that we design, conduct and report research in accordance with recognised standards of scientific competence and ethical good practice. So you are permitted to perform only those tasks for which you are appropriately trained and prepared. We say more about ethics in Chapter 8, when we discuss them in relation to the final-year project.

Interpreting Psychological Data

Observations are our data, but all our observations are theory laden. Sometimes this is difficult to appreciate. We easily forget that when we refer to what we can see, we are only considering a small part of the electromagnetic spectrum (unlike some other animals, we don't see ultra-violet or infra-red, let alone x-rays) and our visual system makes use of gestalt effects so we have a tendency to impose order where there is none.

Beyond problems in our observations, it is rare that all our participants in a study behave in the same way. You wouldn't expect all of your lecturers to get every question on an IQ test correct and your taxi drivers to get every question wrong, but you probably do believe that overall your lecturers have a higher IQ than your taxi drivers. If not, see our section on changing to another university!

What you do find is that there is a *general* effect. So, if you have a group of people who compulsively wash their hands (an example of an obsessive-compulsive disorder), then you would hope that a psychological intervention (like cognitive behavioural therapy, often shortened to CBT) would reduce handwashing for the group. You wouldn't abandon CBT just because one person in a group of 20 actually washed their hands *more*, as long as the other 19 washed their hands *less*. How about if two people got worse? You could make a guess, but we can do more than that by using statistics.

We are usually interested in comparing samples. Usually our samples are the control condition and the experimental condition. In our CBT example, we would want a group who had CBT (experimental condition) and a group who *didn't* have CBT (control condition). Then, any differences between the groups should be due to our intervention: the CBT.

For the two groups, we want to know whether they are from the same or different populations. What does 'same or different populations' mean? It sounds complicated, but really it's just asking whether the two samples are so similar that they could have been taken at random from the same overall population. Think about this. If you chose a group of compulsive handwashers and split them into two groups, there shouldn't be any differences between the groups in how much they handwash. Sure, there may be small differences, but just chance variations. So, those two groups (or samples) come from the same population. But after one group has received CBT and the other hasn't, we would certainly hope that the groups differed in their handwashing, so for handwashing we would expect that the differences between the control and the experimental group would be so large that we would be forced to accept that they now come from different populations.

Formally, we assume that there is no difference between our two samples and any differences between our two samples are due to random, chance variations. This assumption is the 'null hypothesis' (H_0). The 'alternative hypothesis' (H_1) is that there is a difference between the samples. We try to demonstrate the null hypothesis, but if we cannot, we accept the alternative hypothesis (what we're really interested in!). Clearly, you need to select and calculate the inferential statistics correctly. However, just as important is making sure that your conclusions are appropriate. That is, we need to have considered what our results *mean*: you need to think critically about your study.

What are descriptive and inferential statistics?

In psychology, we use both descriptive and inferential statistics:

- *Descriptive* statistics describe our data (typical value and range of data).

- *Inferential* statistics enable us to make inferences (good guesses) about the total population from our sample.

Samples and populations

Descriptive statistics summarise or describe a sample, and inferential statistics generalise from a sample to a general population. We are normally interested in the population rather than the restrictive sample that we've examined. We want to know about human psychology in general, not just the psychology of the few dozen people who took part in our study.

What is a population?

It's easy and useful to think of a population as all the people you might want to study. So, your population might be 'all adults alive right now', but populations could be 'all adult women' or 'all male rats of a certain strain'. However, by 'population' we might mean something a little more abstract, such as a 'population of measures' or scores on an IQ test.

Samples should be randomly chosen from the population that you're interested in. This is easier said than done, as we have to be realistic about what we can do in any study. If we are measuring some human characteristic, we might want to have participants randomly chosen from the world's population, but we probably will accept that we will randomly select from a much smaller pool. Our pool is sometimes psychology students looking for course credit! However, we should always be aware of the biases that can be introduced as a result. Note that samples can be unrepresentative.

Sampling is not a passive process; we need to think critically. One of our favourite examples of this need to think critically is to imagine that you were interested in studying how planes flying bombing missions in the Second World War might best be protected against enemy attack. You might decide to interview the aircrews on their return and ask from which direction they were usually attacked. If most attacks came from underneath the aircraft, then you would probably recommend that more defensive weapons were located there. Unfortunately, you are talking to the wrong people. Who should you talk to? You may have guessed that you need to talk to the aircrews that were shot down. A similar problem occurs if you decide to approach people randomly in the street. This means that you are less likely to sample cyclists and car drivers than those on foot. Perhaps this doesn't matter, but to decide you need to think carefully about what you are trying to achieve and this will have implications for how you select your sample.

So how do we get from a sample to a population?

Here's a simple example. Think of a 'population', for example, height of all adults in the world. Note that our population is *not* the population of the world, but the *height* of all the people in the world (because we're using population in its statistical sense). We can then take a sample from that and measure the height, for example, all of the students in a lecture theatre. We could do the same for other classes of about the same size and the average height would vary from class to class; we call that 'sampling variation'. This sampling variation is related to three things: variability within the sample; the size of the sample; and the proportion of the population covered by the sample. Fortunately, the second is more important than the third. We can then use the following three pieces of information:

- **variability within the sample (usually the standard deviation)**

- **average value of the sample (mean)**

- **number of observations (N)**

and make an 'educated guess' about the population from which the sample came.

But why is that useful?

If we have two samples, we can make an educated guess about how likely (or how probable) it is that both samples come from the same population. We can never be certain that two samples either do come from the same population or that they do not come from the same population. That is what we mean in psychology when we talk about (inferential) statistics.

But why can't we be certain in psychology? I can be certain of lots of things!

Really? You might think so, but let's consider an example: 'The sun will rise tomorrow'. Not unreasonable, and we certainly hope so. But your certainty is based on little more than induction. The sun rose yesterday, and the day before and the day before and the day before ... and so on. However, if the sun suddenly exploded, it wouldn't rise tomorrow. It's unlikely that this will happen, but it certainly isn't impossible – it's just improbable.

Which statistical test should I use?

At undergraduate level there are relatively few statistical tests that you have to understand, so choosing the right one is actually quite easy, *once* you understand your design. Most statistics books have some sort of diagram, usually a flowchart, to help you choose the right statistical test, but we've included a different kind. The version we've produced below contains explanatory text that you can use if you don't find the one in the statistics book helpful for you. However, what you should do as an exercise afterwards is create your own version so that you can quickly write it out in a statistics examination or on a scrap of paper when you are doing your analysis. You do need to be able to do that otherwise you may just be kidding yourself that you understand the choice process.

Box 4:6   Choosing Your Statistical Test

The first question you should ask yourself is whether your data are best thought of as parametric or non-parametric. At undergraduate level, it's safest to assume that data that are in the form of ranks (that is, participants were asked to put their preferences in order from least liked to most liked) are non-parametric and anything else is parametric. Most analyses you'll see reported assume that data are parametric, so that's always the best bet if you aren't sure.

What are you measuring?

There are two types of data that you need to differentiate between when deciding which test to use – data in the form of *categories* or data in the form of *measurement*. Categories are when you are counting the frequency of something, that is, how often it occurs. Measurements are different since you are actually measuring each observation on a scale, not counting it. So:

- If you have data in categories, then you should use the chi-squared (or χ^2) test.

- If you have measurement data, then you need to decide if you are looking at relationships between variables or differences between groups.

When looking at the relationship between variables:

- If you have parametric data, then you should use Pearson's r correlation coefficient.

- If you have non-parametric data, then you should use Spearman's Rho correlation coefficient.

(Continued)

Box 4:6 (Continued)

Examining differences between two groups

The next question is whether the groups are *independent* or *dependent*. That sounds complicated, but actually it isn't. This is just another way of describing designs that are *between-subjects* or *within-subjects*. *Independent groups* means just what it says, that the groups are independent. Crucially, you could change the *order* of the data for that group and it wouldn't be a problem to compare that messed-up data to another set of data. Contrast that with *dependent groups*, where the third piece of data is implicitly paired with the related third piece of data (often because that represents data from the same person). For example, if you were comparing weight before and after a wonderful new diet idea, you would certainly want to compare each person's value *before* the diet with their score *afterwards*. It would be daft to shuffle the data about. So:

- If you have independent groups, you would use the two-sample t-test.

- If you have dependent groups, you would use the related-sample t-test.

However, if your data are most appropriately considered to be non-parametric (see above), then:

- If you have independent groups, you would use the Mann-Whitney U-test.

- If you have dependent groups, you would use the Wilcoxon matched pairs test.

Examining differences between *more than two* groups

Once again, you need to decide if you have *independent* or *dependent* groups, so read through the information above to help you. Then:

- If you have independent groups, you would use ANOVA.

- If you have dependent groups, you would use repeated-measures ANOVA.

Interpreting statistical output

One of the key skills that you need to develop is being able to interpret statistical output. It's easy to think that skill for 'statistics' is being able to use the complicated equations that underlie a statistical test, but that's not the case. Nowadays, when performing a quantitative analysis, researchers will usually input the data into a statistical package like SPSS and click the appropriate buttons to let the computer do the work. However, note the skills that are required:

- **Correctly inputting data in the appropriate format.**

- **Correctly selecting the appropriate test.**

And the next skill is being able to interpret the SPSS output. We don't have the space in this book to explain how to do this for every statistical test and would encourage you to use a book like Howitt and Cramer's *Introduction to SPSS in Psychology* (Prentice Hall, 2004). This book has a specific section for every basic statistical test where they explain how to identify the relevant information from the SPSS output. The book even helps you develop another skill, that of reporting the statistical output in your practical report or dissertation.

How to report statistical tests

It is important to report statistical tests correctly. As a general guide, you need to include:

- **the statistical distribution used**

- **the degrees of freedom (df) or number (N)**

- **the value of the calculation**

- **the probability or significance level.**

For your reports, you need to check that you have supplied the required information clearly and succinctly. It is essential to ensure that you can report the results of your statistical tests *and* it is absolutely essential that you understand what those results actually mean! If in doubt, ask your tutor, and in general it is a good idea to see how results are reported in peer-reviewed published work.

What is the meaning of the 'p-value'?

It is essential to understand p-values. A p-value is just a probability value and tells us *based on the data we've collected and analysed* the probability that the null hypothesis is true. In other words, what is the probability of any differences that we've found being simply down to chance variations? In psychology we decide that if the probability is less than 0.05 (that's 1 in 20), it's so unlikely that differences are due to chance that we'll reject that possibility and accept the alternative hypothesis that the differences are 'real'. If you think about it, trying to reject the null hypothesis is the point of performing the appropriate statistical test.

Box 4:7   Before You Move On …

What is the scientific method?

What are the advantages and disadvantages of experiments and observations?

What are the main contrasts between quantitative and qualitative data?

Sketch out a simple diagram (for example, a flow chart) to enable you to select the correct statistical test.

Find some example SPSS output (for example, on our webpage) for correlation, t-tests and χ^2 tests and identify whether the tests are statistically significant.

When comparing differences between groups, if your p = 0.04, what can you conclude?

5 Teaching Situations

LEARNING OUTCOMES

1. To understand how to prepare to get the most out of your lectures, seminars and practical classes.
2. To be aware of the different kinds of material you will be required to read.
3. To know what is meant by a journal article and how to identify articles you should read.
4. To be aware of techniques that will help you to read and make notes more effectively.

Introduction

During your psychology degree you will participate in a number of different teaching situations. In lectures, you could sit bored as the lecturer drones on and on. In seminars, you could hide in the back of the class hoping that you don't get asked any questions, desperately waiting for the class to end. In practicals, you could wonder what the point of the task is. Why should that be? *Maybe* the lecture is boring and uninspired. *Perhaps* the seminar is too difficult. The practical *might* be inappropriate. Actually, the most likely reason would be that *you* were inadequately prepared.

O
C
R

Box 5:1 Getting the Most from Your Teaching

To get the most out of each teaching situation you must recognise that each teaching and learning event is a series of *communicative* acts. In a lecture, the *communication* may be mostly one way – from the lecturer to you, the student.

(Continued)

> **Box 5:1   (Continued)**
>
> But you have to do your best to understand what the lecturer is trying to get across (otherwise why are you there?), and organising yourself prior to the lecture is the key to success here as elsewhere. In seminars and tutorials, communication should be two-way. You will need to communicate *your* ideas to other students and to the tutor. Again, effective *preparation* is the key. As you progress through the degree, you should find it easier and easier to get more out of each teaching and learning event that you attend. But this will only happen if you build into your approach effective *reflection* on what you have learned and how you might have learned more.

Preparation is Essential

Probably the one thing that can make the biggest difference in how well you do in your psychology degree is how well you prepare for every teaching situation you face. Now, that doesn't mean that you must prepare for every single teaching situation that you attend, but it does mean that the more prepared you are, the better you should do. Of course, you have to do preparation that is effective and we will try to help you do that in this chapter.

Preparing for teaching situations is largely about doing the appropriate background reading. Every session should have some background reading: it could be in the form of reading the relevant chapter from the core text or it might be a specific paper that is recommended. If your unit leader doesn't list any readings for each week, you should ask them to do so.

Effective Reading

Effective reading involves reading the most appropriate material to achieve a specific goal, and reading that material in an efficient way to get the most you can out of your reading in the quickest time. The material you need to read will vary depending on where you are in your degree and on what you have to achieve. Introductory textbooks will probably form a major part of your reading, especially in the first and second years of the course, but as you advance through the degree you should find that you are using textbooks less and less, and reading journal articles more and more. That shift reflects your development as a student, and especially as a critical thinker. General textbooks are very useful when you are starting psychology as they provide a very basic introduction to all areas of psychology. Area-specific textbooks, for example on cognitive psychology, are even better as they normally provide more detail on relevant studies and explore some of the complexities. Even better than those are topic-specific text-books, which provide overviews of particular aspects of a specific topic, for example 'memory' or 'attention'. However, for the most up-to-date and rigorous material you should be looking at recently published journal articles on the topic in which you are interested. Doing so will enable you to be aware of what the *current* controversies are and to appreciate the detail on individual experiments.

To use journal articles most efficiently, it is essential that you are able to read them effectively. Below we provide a specific example of one way to read a journal article, but first let's consider reading for your degree.

What is a journal article?

Research psychologists publish the results of their research in the form of papers (or articles) in journals. Journals can be general and publish papers on many different areas of psychology, for example, *Psychological Review*. But they can also be very specific and publish papers on a very restricted part of psychology, for example, the journal *Visual Perception* publishes articles only on, well – visual perception. In the main, papers that appear in journals are peer reviewed. This means that prior to being accepted for publication they have been read by other experts in the field who have made a judgement on the originality and quality of the paper. We also refer to this process of peer review as 'refereeing'. Very often, when a paper is first submitted, the referees will request that various changes are made before the paper can be published. They may even ask that additional empirical work is undertaken. Papers can also be rejected for publication, and in the most prestigious journals the rejection rate can be very high.

Think about why you are reading

The first thing we want you to consider is *why* you are reading. There are four main reasons why you may be reading something as part of your degree:

- **preparation for a lecture**

- **specific reading set for a seminar**

- **writing an assignment**

- **revising for an examination**

These are examined in detail below.

Reading before a lecture

The first, and obvious, question is 'What should I read?'. Your lecturer may give you set reading to do; if you are not given pre-assigned reading, then you should read the relevant chapter of the core textbook for the unit. The next question to consider is 'Why should I read?'. Lectures involve listening to someone talk; even when the lecturer is very good, you may miss a link between ideas and get lost. So it's good to have done some preparatory reading and to have used that reading to sketch out for yourself, for example:

- **an overview of the topic of the lecture**

- **illustrations of concepts that are especially important**

- **illustrations of experiments or other empirical studies that are especially pertinent to the topic.**

You've almost certainly already discovered that it is easier to understand difficult ideas if they are not completely unfamiliar to you. It's very frustrating if you are in a lecture and you find the material too difficult to understand and end up getting lost. If that happens, it becomes extremely difficult to make good notes and the notes that you do take are likely to be a confused attempt to produce a verbatim copy.

Good preparation prior to a lecture involves your trying to form a mental map or schema of material relevant to the topic of the lecture. It is much easier to understand new material if you can organise it and fit it into an existing knowledge-base – no matter how small that existing knowledge-base is. So, make a note of:

- **definitions of any new 'technical' terms**

- **major concepts**

- **key experiments (or other empirical studies)**

- **key disputes/disagreements about the topic area.**

Also take the time to formulate some questions. If you cannot formulate any questions, that is a very good indication that you haven't properly engaged with the material.

Additionally, during the lecture make sure that the lecturer answers them; if they have not been answered, ask the lecturer afterwards.

Reading before a seminar

More so than reading before a lecture, the reading you do before a seminar depends on the nature of the seminar. It may be useful to do something similar to reading prior to a lecture, although you are likely to have been given specific reading to enable you to contribute to a specific seminar task. But you may also find, particularly at level 3, that *you* have to decide what to read. If that is so, you need to consider whether you will have to address the specific questions or tasks set for the seminar. The more specific the questions, the more specific you need your reading to be. Alternatively, you may be required to give more general responses to an important theoretical issue. You may even be required to prepare an oral presentation that will be delivered either informally to a small group or formally to the whole seminar. We will provide some further guidance on making oral presentations in Chapter 6.

Reading for a coursework assignment

The value of reading for a lecture or seminar is hopefully apparent from the previous two sections (though it is disappointingly uncommon for students to do this). However, all students know that you need to read to enable you to complete your assignments. Reading for an assignment requires a wider range of reading than for a lecture or seminar. You should be given a *starting point* for your reading by your lecturer. If you are lucky, the lecturer may even supply a photocopy of a relevant paper or book chapter, or may simply give you the reference(s) and let you track down the appropriate material. But do remember that material is just a starting point, a bare minimum for you to do.

Tailor your reading to the assignment topic

A good place to start is from a relevant textbook chapter, but be prepared to look at more than one textbook, as doing so can often provide different viewpoints on the same material. It's also useful to use a dictionary of psychology to ensure that you understand exactly what is meant by specific terms such as 'attitudes' or 'cognition'. It is important to recognise that if you only read one chapter in one textbook, you are limiting how well you can do. After all, you can only really report back what the text says. If you do that, you are likely to restrict your maximum mark to a lower second.

Reading for an examination

During the semester, you need steadily to build up a body of notes and of key reading materials to assist you in your revision – it's no good leaving everything for the revision period. That's pretty obvious, but requires real discipline and organisation. Before you move on to the next paragraph, think about how you might do it. Take out your exam timetable if you have one and think when you could create such lists for each of your subjects.

Did you allow for work on assignments, preparation for lectures/seminars? Did you also allow for any part-time work, family commitments and personal time? It's easy to think that you can squeeze work in, but none of us are good at making sure we get things done if it's not urgent. Don't try to do your examination preparation when the teaching has finished!

A good strategy is to decide well ahead of the examination period on which broad areas you are going to concentrate. You may find it useful to look at past papers from previous examinations, but check with the lecturer that the topics being covered haven't changed. Then you can read with those particular topics/broad questions in mind. Keeping a record of what you read is vital, but each person will develop their own method of doing this (we'll give you some tips later).

I've read the textbooks – where now?

If you've done your reading properly you should already know! But some tips are:

- **Have a look at the 'further reading' sections at the end of textbook chapters.**

- **Follow up the references to specific journal papers in the textbook chapters you have read that the author has identified as especially important.**

- **Then follow up references to further specific articles in those journal papers.**

And so on and on and on and on … In general, you should expect to do more reading as you progress through the degree. It should get easier to read academic work as you go through the degree, as long as you have put in the effort in your earlier years. Like many things, the more you do it, the better you get! Having said that, don't forget the unit material that you've been given by the lecturer(s) and, hopefully, your lecture notes should be a great help. We say more about making the most of lectures later in this chapter.

Think about what you are reading

You could be reading any of the following:

- **textbook chapter**

- **journal paper**

- **theoretical or empirical report**

- **monograph (book, short or long, on a specific topic).**

Think about where you are reading

You might be reading in the university library or at home, maybe in an Internet café or even on public transport on the way home. Are these equally suitable for your purpose? Obviously not; some of these will be noisy and some of these are less suited to making notes. You should try really hard to make sure that you can finish the reading task you set yourself in the time you have available.

Why is preparation important?

Your reading must be effective. If you don't know why you are doing it, or you are doing it in a place that is not appropriate for your purpose, then your reading time is likely to be wasted. Think about times when you've read something but haven't really been focused; at the end it's possible to not have a clue what it was you were reading, which is a complete waste of time and is very dispiriting. So, reading on public transport can be good for some purposes, for example, getting an overview of a topic via a textbook chapter, but you will not be able to look up things you don't understand or easily make notes.

One Method for Effective Reading and Note-taking – SQ3R

Below we demonstrate one way to effectively read and take notes on a journal article. In this case we've chosen:

Ward, T. (2000). Sexual offenders' cognitive distortions as implicit theories. *Aggression and Violent Behavior, 5*, 491–507. You will get more out of this section of the book if you can obtain a copy of this article. You will be able to do this easily from the Internet if your university subscribes to this journal. Otherwise order it through the inter-library loan system (see Chapter 7 on using libraries if you don't know how to do this).

Step one: SURVEY the material

Read the title and read the abstract if there is one (that may be all you need to do!). Then, pay attention to the format of the material. For example, what are the headings and subheadings? These can contain useful information about the direction of the author's argument. Do remember to pay attention to graphics – diagrams, graphs, tables and charts – as these are there to convey information concisely. See how much you can understand from these before you start reading the text itself.

Read the introduction and/or summary, conclusion or discussion to get an overview of what the material is about and of the author's purposes. Concentrate on explicit statements of aims and points that the author indicates are important. The author may even tell you that an idea is important. Key ideas will usually be explicitly discussed in the introduction and conclusion (of each section as well as of the whole).

Pay attention to any reading aids the author has given. Remember, we put these in because we think they help the reader (and research confirms that they do). So watch out for:

- **bold or italic print**

- **learning outcomes at the beginning**

- **interim summaries**

- **boxes to discuss particular concepts/debates**

- **self-study questions.**

Step two: Ask QUESTIONS

Don't start to read in more detail with an empty mind! Think about what you know about the topic already. You might be surprised by how much you already know. Think about the questions you want answered by reading the material you have selected. If you don't have any, then *why* are you reading it? For each section, think about what questions the section headings raise.

Now, let's look at that example. Let's start with the title of the journal article: 'Sexual offenders' cognitive distortions as implicit theories'. This should prompt a number of questions:

- **What kind of sexual offenders is the author writing about?**

- **What is meant by a cognitive distortion?**

- **What is an implicit theory?**

Here's the abstract:

In this article, I argue that sexual offenders' cognitive distortions emerge from underlying causal theories about the nature of their victims. These implicit theories function like scientific theories and are used to explain empirical regularities (e.g., other people's actions) and to make predictions about the world. They are relatively coherent and constituted by a number of interlocking ideas and their component concepts and categories. Following a review of research from other areas in psychology on implicit theories, I consider implications of this perspective for understanding cognitive distortions in offenders as implicit theories.

What questions arise for you having read the abstract? Perhaps questions such as these:

- **What sexual offenders is the author going to talk about?**

- **What is a cognitive distortion?**

- **Implicit theories are like scientific theories in that they are used to explain empirical regularities and make predictions – are they the same in any other way?**

- **Why are the theories implicit?**

- **What is a scientific theory?**

- **What is a causal theory?**

Perhaps you can answer some of these before you start, perhaps not. Be aware!

Here are some more questions:

- **A scientific theory is an explicit theory – someone expresses it and writes it down! So what might an implicit (scientific) theory be?**

- **There's research on implicit theories in other areas of psychology – which areas?**

- **What are the clinical implications of this way of looking at sex offenders?**

At this point you may decide to read no further. For example, imagine that you were writing an essay that asked you to evaluate the effectiveness of drugs in the treatment of sexual offenders. Just reading the abstract will tell you the paper is not relevant (if the title hadn't already done so). But if you were writing an essay discussing the influence of cognitive psychology on clinical psychology you might be tempted to read on, especially if you had decided to use sex offenders for a case study as an illustration of influence.

You should have noted down headings and subheadings in your initial survey:

- COGNITIVE DISTORTIONS IN SEXUAL OFFENDERS
    - Schema Construct
- IMPLICIT THEORIES IN PSYCHOLOGY
- SEXUAL OFFENDERS IMPLICIT THEORIES
    - Examples of Implicit Theories in Sexual Offenders
    - Cognitive Distortions as Process
    - Offender Type
    - Implicit Theory Acquisition and Development
- CONCLUSIONS

The headings give you a way to organise your note-taking (we'll say more on this in a moment). They show you where you will get the answers to some of your questions. They also raise more questions!

- **What is a schema construct?**

- **Cognitive distortion as a process – a process as opposed to what?**

At this point you might start panicking as the questions start to mount up. You might have thought that reading would answer questions, not produce more and more. *But*, this shows that not understanding something should not cause you to panic – it is the beginning of wisdom if you use it to your advantage. Asking specific questions is actually a sign that you are engaging with the material and that is how you can get to understand it.

Step three: starting to read

Now, and only now, can you start to read the paper in earnest. Read the introduction and/or summary, conclusion or discussion to get an overview of what the material is about and of the author's purposes. The penultimate paragraph of the introduction to the article we are using as an example summarises the argument of the paper!

It should already be clear that you don't read by starting at the first page and then ploughing through the material one page at a time – you don't (have to) read psychology the way you would read a novel.

Let's try reading just the first sentence of each paragraph, for instance. (N.B. There are other strategies, for example, reading the first and last paragraph of each section first).

> Researchers and clinicians have often been struck by the distorted way in which sexual offenders describe and justify their offending behavior.
>
> While considerable attention has been paid to documenting the content of the cognitive distortions in sexual offenders … relatively few researchers have grappled with the issue of their underlying structure or nature.
>
> I suggest that in the sexual offending area, and the broader domain of psychopathology research and theory, the received view is that distorted thoughts and attitudes arise from underlying maladaptive assumptions or beliefs.
>
> An additional problem concerns the origins of these cognitive distortions or maladaptive schema.
>
> In this article, I argue that sexual offender's cognitive distortions emerge from underlying causal theories about the nature of their victims rather than stemming from unrelated, independent beliefs.
>
> There is little doubt that various cognitive activities, maladaptive beliefs, and distorted thinking, play an important role in sexual offending.
>
> Examples of cognitive distortions frequently found in child molesters include: 'children often initiate sex and know what they want' … .
>
> Rapists' beliefs, on the other hand, tend to center on issues of responsibility … .
>
> Concerning cognitive processes, research supports the notion that sexual offenders interpret sexual information in maladaptive ways ….

Continue for yourself – but we think that you get the point. Beginning like this means that you can quickly tell if the paper is going to be useful for your purpose. You begin to get an answer to some of your questions and you begin to get some structure to your note-taking. If you do all this, you should have a basic structure for your reading. Now read each section in turn – recall your questions and see which of them you can answer (new questions will, of course, arise also). But don't be lazy or anxious to rush ahead. That's very tempting, but it doesn't work so you actually end up wasting your time.

Step four: RECITE what you have learned

After each section recall your questions and see if you can answer them from memory. Perhaps write a short summary of the section from memory. Don't go on until you can do this. You might think you don't need to as you may feel that you could answer those questions if you wanted. Really? Well, it shouldn't take more than a moment to write down a few words of an answer so do it *now*. If you did actually do it, you might have found it a little harder than you thought and found that you had to go back and quickly re-read some part of the paper.

Step five: REVIEW what you have read

Go back over all your questions to see if you have answers. See what new questions you have that you can't answer from the paper. You will need to find the answer elsewhere, perhaps in one of the sources that are listed in this paper's reference section. Make sure you have a clear record of what you have learned from the paper.

So, as we said earlier, this process is known as the SQ3R system of reading:

SURVEY
QUESTION
READ
RECITE
REVIEW

The obvious, very natural response is that 'This looks like a lot of effort – I can just read the material through from beginning to end and get what I need.' Fine, if you say so. But reading without understanding is pointless and it wastes time because you just have to go back and read the material again, and again, and again … if you don't approach the task systematically. Remember, your aim is to 'work smart', not 'work hard'; you need your efforts to be effective.

Taking notes on your reading

Some ideas for note-taking should be apparent from the example above. Focus on questions and answers, not just simple transcription where you are trying to write everything down. Similarly, if you like to use a highlighter pen and find that you are turning the pages yellow, pink and green, you might want to consider whether that's an effective way of reading. Ensure that you write structured notes that are based on your questions. Go back over your notes when you think you have finished and ask yourself whether they make sense. Do they assist you to complete your task? If not, then you need to go through the material again. You might like to look at other general study skills material for other ways of taking notes. For example, some people find 'mind maps' a useful way of organising material. Likewise, some people like to keep an index card record where they can list major points and major empirical studies. Doing so can be a great help when revising as well as completing an assessment.

How to Focus During Teaching Situations

'Phew! That preparatory reading is a lot of work, but at least it means that I can doze during the lectures.' Sadly, that's not the case. Reading before teaching is extremely valuable (if done effectively), but it's preparation and you now need to think about how best to focus during the teaching situation. To do that, you need to think *why* you are there and *what* you are trying to achieve. Let's consider the different teaching situations.

Lectures

Lectures are the clichéd university experience: a large hall with tiered seating and a lecturer at the front talking. But think why we have lectures. Lectures are actually a very effective way to communicate a general overview of a topic to large numbers of people, for example, the key concepts that are used in discussions of the topic, the main theories on the topic and the important evidence that we have for evaluating those theories. You need to think about how you can best understand and take notes on that kind of material. The most general advice to give is that you shouldn't be trying to take down everything the lecturer says. This is impossible, for one thing, and reveals a lack of thought about what a lecture is and what you intend to do with the information after the lecture. You also need to tailor your note-taking to the aids that a lecturer should use to help you understand. For instance, it is increasingly common for lecturers to use PowerPoint presentations and to provide you with copies of the slides (either to use in the lecture or after the lecture to help you review what you have learned and revise for examinations).

Having handouts does make your life a lot easier, but you shouldn't think that it means you don't need to attend or that you don't need to think about note-taking. With regard to attendance, notice that a typical handout will only take a few minutes to read, but the lecture itself will often be an hour long. The reason for this discrepancy is that the handout will concentrate on key bullet points, but in the lecture itself the lecturer will explain and illustrate these main points, and ideally getting a sense of whether the students understand what is being said. As a lecturer, if you see lots of puzzled faces, you try to give more examples or think of a different way of explaining a theory. You also can be asked questions and hopefully give useful answers. If you don't attend, you miss out on all that. The other problem with not attending when there are lecture handouts is what actually happens as a result. Every lecture we give has someone taking an extra handout for a friend. But what happens to those handouts? Does the person who doesn't attend work through that material before the next lecture? Do they look up the relevant references? Do they make further notes? Do they see the lecturer during their tutorial hours to ask them any questions that arose? The vast majority of those handouts are put straight into a folder and only get looked at in the week before the examination. We're often amused by students complaining after examinations that the lecture handouts were too brief – they're always the students who we don't recognise as attending our lectures!

Lecture handouts are often available before the lecture starts, and may even be available beforehand on your department's webpages. You should try to get a copy as soon as possible so that you can have a quick read through. It should help with your preparatory reading if you can get the handout, as while you are reading you can make notes and identify any questions you have. Otherwise, during the lecture you should try to *think* about what is being said, constantly thinking of questions that you might have. It is here that you benefit from the preparatory reading as you should have a basic understanding of the material and so can check that your understanding is correct and also spot any gaps in your understanding, which the lecture may well fill. Be prepared to ask questions; lecturers like questions as it suggests that someone is awake! But some of the questions you might want to ask the lecturer afterwards, or even during the break in the lecture (if there is one).

We started this chapter by saying that students sometimes find lectures to be boring. However, if you do the appropriate preparation and have a strategy for how you are going to work in the lecture, you may well find that your lectures start becoming a lot more interesting. Give it a go and see!

Once the lecture is over you may be tempted to pack your notes away and, well, never look at them again, or dig them out only when you come to revise and find that they make no sense to you at all. So, after the lecture you need to build in time to *reflect* on what you have learned in the lecture. Try to write a one-page summary of the key points, using your notes for guidance. Look back at the questions that arose during your preparatory reading and check that they have been answered. If they haven't, perhaps you need to go back and re-read that material. You might also reflect on whether this is a topic that interests you a great deal, or is of only peripheral interest. If the former, then you might decide to undertake further reading and research on the topic to begin building up the body of information that you will need to answer a coursework or exam question on this topic. You can't possibly work at every topic to the same extent, so if the topic of the lecture doesn't interest you, perhaps you need do no more – but do be sure that the topic isn't a required part of the assessment for the unit before you do this.

Can I record the lecture?

Most lecturers don't mind if you do this (but do ask first) and some students are specifically permitted to record lectures (for example, if they find note-taking difficult because of dyslexia). But if you do this, you should recognise that the recording is not a substitute for note-taking since you will have to replay the lecture and take notes on it later. Sadly, there are *no* short cuts!

Seminars

Seminars are another important teaching situation. Often, units will have both lectures and seminars; the idea is that the lecture introduces the theories and key studies, and the seminars provide an opportunity to explore those theories and studies in a more active manner. Your lecturers may tell you that the best seminars are the ones where they do little talking; they are there for 'crowd control' as the students are very engaged with the material. Unfortunately, seminars are sometimes hampered by the number of students who haven't done the background reading (and may not have attended the lecture), who as a result don't really have anything to say. It really is essential to do the background reading as seminars provide a fantastic opportunity to engage with the material with an academic who can guide you, but only if you have done the reading.

Do try to make notes during a seminar, but try also to keep them short. Note down any insights that you, or someone else, have. Again, note down new words or phrases or 'good questions' that the seminar tutor identifies. It's useful to bear in mind the specific aim of each seminar. For example, the seminar might be called 'Stereotypes', but you will find that the aim is to understand specific aspects of stereotypes, so you should bear those in mind when you are engaging with the tasks. Also, do remember that the seminar tutor is there to answer questions, so make use of the opportunity. And remember that there is usually some time at the end of the session to ask one or two (brief) questions on a one-to-one basis.

Practicals

Psychology degrees involve a reasonable amount of practical work. The same principles apply here as for seminars. You should identify and remember the aim of the session, do appropriate preparatory reading and make *brief* notes throughout.

Tutorials

The other teaching situation that you should encounter is one-to-one tutorials (sometimes two- or maybe three-to-one). Your lecturers should have weekly tutorial hours in which you can book an appointment. Do make use of these when they are available, as we find that we can help students a great deal in just a few minutes if they come with a particular question. The big problem is that they usually don't come! If you do make an appointment, ensure that you turn up slightly early (to allow for delays) and make sure that you have an agenda – a clear sense of what you want to achieve. We say more about one-on-one tutorials in Chapter 8. If you have 'more than one'-to-one tutorials, then you are very lucky as such teaching is very useful. However, once again, *you* need to ensure that you are properly prepared so that you have something to say and don't just sit there nervously.

But I'm scared to talk to the lecturer!

Coming to university can be intimidating. You may think that you know nothing about a topic and that the lecturer knows far, far more. Well, we'd hope that lecturers know a lot more about psychology than you, but isn't that the point? You are at university to learn from the lecturers, but that doesn't mean that you know nothing. You will almost certainly have skills that your lecturers don't have, such as ability to play a musical instrument, a fluent second language or good dress sense. Lecturers have friends and family who don't know anything about their topic, but they don't think less of them. Some lecturers do have an arrogant air and can be extremely intimidating. However, ask yourself why they feel the need to project such an image. Like school bullies, it's often because they themselves are afraid so they create a character to hide behind. So, remember that the arrogant lecturer should be a source of curiosity, not fear!

After teaching

'Hooray! Now off to the pub.' That might be the usual reaction after teaching, of the teaching staff, but *you* need to do a little more. It is difficult to review each teaching experience, but it should make revision far easier if you've tied up the loose ends. You need to ensure that you have understood all the key concepts and if you haven't, that you make an appointment to discuss those problems. It's important to do your review while the teaching is still in your mind, so try to put aside some time in the evening after your teaching sessions to write up your notes and do any follow-up reading.

Final Thought

We've suggested doing 'more' work than you might usually. We've recommended doing preparatory reading in a very structured way, rather than reading through quickly. We've suggested ways to make the most of your time in teaching situations and we've stressed the importance of 'debriefing' yourself after teaching. However, if you do this, not only should you get higher marks in your assessments, but you should find that revision is far less stressful and mysteriously more effective. It is *your* decision as to how you work, but remember: work *smart*, not *hard*.

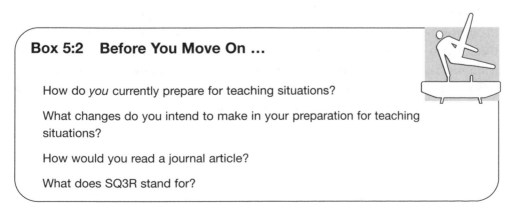

Box 5:2 Before You Move On …

How do *you* currently prepare for teaching situations?

What changes do you intend to make in your preparation for teaching situations?

How would you read a journal article?

What does SQ3R stand for?

6 Assessments

LEARNING OUTCOMES

1. To be able to organise yourself effectively to succeed in your psychology assessments.
2. To be aware of some strategies that will help you to write better coursework and examination essays.
3. To understand what makes a good practical report.
4. To be able to use feedback you receive on your work effectively.
5. To be able to reference your work correctly and avoid plagiarism.
6. To be aware of the requirements of some other forms of assessment, including short-answer examinations, multiple-choice examinations, oral presentations and posters.

Introduction

You will probably find that this chapter is the one you turn to most often, as it contains information about how to do assessments as painlessly and effectively as possible. You will probably need to come back to this chapter again and again as you progress through the degree because you will find that you need to focus on slightly different skills for the different levels of assessment. Here we provide guidance for a wide range of different assessments, but we leave specific help for the project to the next chapter. If you follow our OCR strategy in completing your assessment tasks, you will find that you have a greater chance of achieving your full potential.

> ### Box 6:1 Using OCR in Assessments
>
> It really is true that you can perform better in your assessments if you *organise* your time and effort effectively. It doesn't matter how good you are at psychology if you leave yourself with too much to do in too short a time. It really is true that essays and practical reports are *acts of communication* between you and the markers. All of the principles of good communication that we discus throughout this book apply to your writing. It really is true that you will only improve as you proceed through your course if you take the time to *reflect* on what you have written before you hand it in, and *reflect* on the feedback you are given on your previous work.

Although the assessments we will discuss are varied, ranging from essays to practical reports and oral presentations, the most important thing for you to do is to be organised and not to leave things until the last minute. Also, remember that academic staff usually have to mark a large numbers of assessments in a relatively limited time, so do all you can to help them (and keep them in a good mood). Poorly organised work that is over the word limit with lots of spelling mistakes and grammatical errors takes far more time to grade and does not get high marks! Tutors really do prefer to give out high marks for good work that can be marked without the tutor having to make lots of corrections.

You arc likely to think that assessment is the most important and stressful part of your degree programme. In some respects this is obviously correct as your performance in assessments will determine your final mark. Yet it is wrong to isolate assessment from other aspects of your degree experience. We will discuss in a moment how the stress related to assessments can be reduced by effective self-management (see the section 'Organising for Success' below). But it is also important that you see that regular attendance at lectures, and the systematic completion of seminar tasks and other non-assessed work – such as reading associated with classes – can contribute to success in your assessments. You should be assessed on material that is covered in your classes, so working systematically and consistently throughout your course should mean that you have to hand most of the resources (notes, summaries of key articles, experiments and book chapters) you need when you come to write your assignments or prepare for your exams.

Organising for Success

We are going to discuss organising for success first, since if you are not organised, all the guidance in the world on completing assessments will be futile. Remember, organisation is the first step of OCR.

Most university departments of psychology will publish an assessment schedule at the beginning of each year or semester that will set out the deadline by which you have to hand in coursework. Examination weeks should also be scheduled, so you will have a good idea of the amount of revision time that you have after teaching has finished. You should make sure that you obtain this information as soon as possible.

Coursework

The key thing to recognise at the outset is that the coursework assessment schedule provides you with a *deadline*, not a hand-in date. A deadline is the last day on which you can submit the work for full marks (unless you have what are normally called mitigating circumstances or an extension), not the day that you are required to hand in the work. You need to *take control* and *plan* your own assessment schedule to ensure that you do not find yourself with lots of work to complete as deadlines approach. Students often complain to lecturers that coursework deadlines should be scheduled differently from the way they are. These complaints rightly cut no ice. It is part and parcel of modern university life that students learn to manage their workloads (as you will have to do when in employment). So once you know your coursework assessment deadlines, get out your diary or calendar and make a realistic plan of how you intend to complete the required work in good time.

Box 6:2 Planning Your Work Schedule

Take some time out now to work out how long you think you will need to complete, for example, a 2,000-word essay.

What factors did you consider? You should have factored in time for gathering material (perhaps you will have to travel to a library off-campus, or make time to do some research on the Internet). Then you have to think about the time needed to read, re-read and summarise the material you have gathered (see Chapter 5). Finally, how long did you allocate for planning the essay (see 'Writing Essays', p. 67), for drafting it and for reading and redrafting it (see 'Drafting and redrafting', p. 74)? As different people will work at different speeds and in different ways, it is not possible to give a definitive view on how much time writing a 2,000-word essay will take. But one thing we do know is that people in general are over-optimistic when they assess how long a task will take. Psychologists have conducted careful studies on many areas of life (including students planning to meet assessment deadlines) that reveal this 'over-optimistic bias' (as it is called). Indeed, people remain over-optimistic even when they are fully aware that they tend to fail to meet their planned deadlines! This means that you must plan to take account of circumstances that you do not foresee when you plan – you need the time equivalent of a rainy day fund that you can draw upon when the unforeseen happens and you get behind your schedule. If you do this, then it will not be a disaster if you fall behind your planned schedule.

Examinations

As with coursework, you need to *plan* your revision in light of the specific details of your university's academic calendar. Check how much time you have between the end of the teaching period and the dates of the examinations you have to sit. This will tell you what your effective revision period will be. For some universities this can be as little as *one week*, but it may be more, especially if there is a vacation immediately at the end of a teaching period. Obviously, the more time you have between the end of teaching and your examinations, the easier it is to plan and execute your revision (though remember that if those weeks include vacation, then some of your time will inevitably be taken up with vacation activities!).

Let us stress again here that it is a mistake to isolate revision from the rest of your learning experiences. You do learn many things in your studies that are not examined, but you are very unlikely to be examined on topics that have not been covered in your lectures, seminars and practical classes or that are not included in the published learning outcomes for the unit. Your studies should also not be solely aimed at completing assessment tasks. But with these provisos, it is worth keeping in mind, from the very start of each examined course unit or module, the examination you will ultimately have to take. In a slogan: revise from day one!

What does this mean in practice? It means thinking ahead. It means understanding that you should revise from notes that you take throughout the course (see Chapter 5) – lecture notes, notes on seminar activities, notes on chapters you have read in textbooks and monographs and notes on key journal papers. If you have not taken the time to get these in order prior to your revision period, you are likely to struggle.

You also need to think ahead about the examination paper itself. Be sure that you know the number of questions that you have to answer, and the number of question choices you are given. Also make sure that you know whether the exam has sections with a requirement that at least one question is answered in each section. And, of course, make sure you know how long you are given to answer the examination paper. You need to ensure that you can answer all required questions. Failing to do that is the easiest way to fail the examination itself. This means that you need to revise more topics than you will actually use in the examination, since you will have to anticipate the possibility that a topic you revise does not appear on a particular year's exam or the possibility that you can't answer the particular question set on one of your revised topics.

Once you are clear on your topics, then you need to think about the nature of the questions that are likely to be set by your lecturers. Past examination papers are an essential resource here since they are a guide to the topics that will be examined and to the style of question that is set. You should, however, check that the course unit has not fundamentally changed since the past papers were set. If that has happened, or if the course is new and there are no – or only one or two – past papers, then you need to ask your lecturer for guidance. Lecturers will be prepared to do this.

As it is impossible to prepare an answer to every possible question that might be set, you need to do some topic selection and direct your preparation and revision to them. It is tempting to select topics on the basis of difficulty, that is, to select those topics you think are less difficult. This is a mistake. You are probably not a good judge of this and, in our experience, students often think that a topic is easy simply because they haven't understood it. If you want a simple rule of thumb – choose topics that you enjoy or find interesting.

Once you have selected your topics and you are settling down to revise, think ahead again. You will have to answer specific questions in the examination. It is vital that you come to view revision as a creative process, not a process of rote learning. A fundamental mistake that many students make is to think that they can answer an exam question by simply regurgitating everything they can remember on the topic of the question. This strategy will not be a successful one. You will only obtain good marks if you answer the specific question set. So organise your revision around key debates and controversies on the topics you have selected. For example, don't try to rote learn the results of a key experiment. Frame the experiment within a relevant debate and formulate a view on how its results impact on that debate. Similarly, don't try to rote learn the definition of a key term or concept. Figure out what role the concept plays in discussion of your topic and formulate a view on the usefulness or otherwise of the concept. If you revise in this way, you will find that you will be much less likely to be taken by surprise by a question. This way of revising is more fun as well as more effective. If you are worried about remembering what you revise – and hence are tempted by rote learning – don't be! We know from psychological studies of human memory that we remember things better when we organise what we have to remember in meaningful ways.

Finally, a key part of the revision process is writing practice essays. You might choose to do this at first with your notes to guide you and with no time pressure. But remember that in the examination you will usually not have notes and you will be under time pressure. It is a good idea, therefore, to do some practice that simulates examination conditions. Indeed, there is a psychological principle known as 'the encoding specificity principle'. Essentially, this principle states that we find it easier to recall information in a context that appropriately matches the environment in which that information was learned. Hence, if some of your learning is done under exam conditions, it should assist your subsequent retrieval of information in the examination.

You might also consider revising with colleagues on your course for some of the time. This can be fun and is made easier by the revision methods we have outlined. And if you are revising with colleagues, read one another's practice essays and provide friendly but honest criticism of them.

Writing Essays

You have organised your time, and you are now sitting down in front of a blank computer screen or examination script and have to deliver the goods. Good organisation can only take you so far!

Communication

Here is our simple message about what to write. Writing is an *act of communication* (second part of OCR) between you and your audience or reader. It is an attempt to convince your audience, by giving reasons and evidence, of the view you have come to on the question you are answering. You must give up entirely the idea that writing essays or exam answers involves dumping onto paper everything you know about a topic. When you write something you must:

- **make your contribution as informative as is required but no more than that**

- **be relevant**

- **avoid obscurity**

- **avoid ambiguity**

- **be orderly.**

These guidelines follow Grice's maxims of conversation as given in Grice P. (1989). *Studies in the Way of Words*. Cambridge, MA: Harvard University Press.

We will give you guidance on how to do all this as we proceed in this chapter. But first: stop, for a moment, and think about your audience – the person with whom you are communicating. Who is your audience?

Your essays will usually be read and marked by your lecturers (typically one of the people who has taught the unit). But you *must not* make the mistake of thinking that you *needn't* explain something because – of course – the lecturer knows what a concept involves, or knows how an experiment works. In an essay you have to demonstrate what *you* know. One useful method is to think of your audience as an educated layperson who knows the basics of how science works, but who has little or no knowledge of the specific topic you are writing about.

We have mentioned already that you will always be answering a specific question. The reader will want a clear statement of *your* answer to the question and why *you* think your answer is correct. So don't start writing until you have formed a view, even if only a preliminary one, on what the essay title is asking you to do. Indeed, you can transform this into the major aim of your essay. You will find that some words appear again and again in essay titles, and it is worth spending a little time thinking about these.

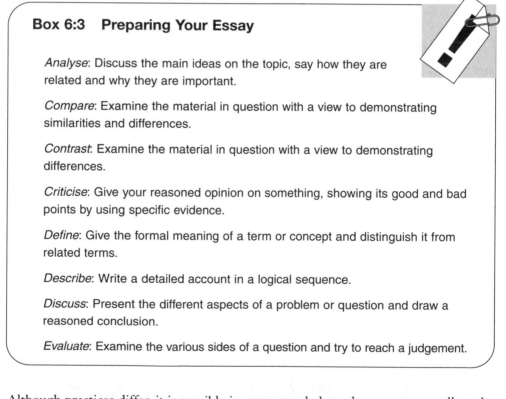

Box 6:3   Preparing Your Essay

Analyse: Discuss the main ideas on the topic, say how they are related and why they are important.

Compare: Examine the material in question with a view to demonstrating similarities and differences.

Contrast: Examine the material in question with a view to demonstrating differences.

Criticise: Give your reasoned opinion on something, showing its good and bad points by using specific evidence.

Define: Give the formal meaning of a term or concept and distinguish it from related terms.

Describe: Write a detailed account in a logical sequence.

Discuss: Present the different aspects of a problem or question and draw a reasoned conclusion.

Evaluate: Examine the various sides of a question and try to reach a judgement.

Although practices differ, it is possible in many psychology departments to talk to the lecturer who has set the essay questions before embarking on your essay. If this opportunity is available, you should take advantage of it. It is a good way to avoid going off on completely the wrong track.

Structure

The guidance given in this section applies to both coursework essays and examination essays. It should be stressed again that we can only give *guidance*. There are many ways to write a good essay, and you should strive to find your own voice. But if you follow our advice, you should be on the right track.

Essays must be structured. If they are not structured, you will fail to communicate effectively. You will, for instance, fail to be orderly and fail to include all of the relevant information. This means essays must have parts that are linked together. The three basic parts of an essay are:

- **the introduction**

- **the main body of the essay (which will often have sub-parts)**

- **the conclusion.**

What about essay plans?

Essay plans are very useful both for examinations and for coursework, as they remind you of important points that you need to cover in your essay. If you look at our detailed contents list, you will see that it is a type of essay plan – we could use it to ensure that we covered all the topics we wanted to in a particular chapter. In examinations, sketching out an essay plan ensures that you will be able to complete the essay and not suddenly realise that there is an important gap in your knowledge. It's also a reassuring way to scribble down some key references so that you don't have to worry about your mind going blank at a crucial moment. In coursework, you can steadily develop your essay plan as you read more material and take notes. If you produce your essay plan on a word-processing package, then it's easier to insert new material and re-order material in a very tidy and time efficient way.

The introduction

The introduction should provide a context for your essay. It might, for example, inform the reader why the question you are answering is important, and it might indicate the scope of your essay informing the reader of what aspects of the topic you intend to cover and why. It might briefly review some of the major positions that have been taken on the question. But don't write an historical review of any and every idea on the topic. Be relevant!

The introduction should also present the reader with an outline map of what is to come. Make sure that your introduction is not vacuous. Too often students introduce their essays like this:

> First the topic of the essay will be introduced, then some major theories will be considered then a conclusion will be provided.

Suppose you are writing an essay in answer to the question, 'What are the clinical implications of recent work on cognitive distortions in sexual offenders?' A better introduction would be:

> The main thrust of this essay will be to argue that recent work on cognitive distortions can be shown to have little relevance for clinical practice with most types of sexual offender. First, the recent literature on cognitive distortions in sexual offenders will be briefly considered and core themes identified. Second, a selective report of relevant research on the clinical evaluation of therapies based on this work will be outlined. It will be argued that this research suggests that … Finally, I will briefly discuss the reasons why the clinical implications of work on cognitive distortions has been so disappointing, and briefly outline two alternative approaches that seem to offer more assistance to clinicians.

The main body

The main body of the essay must work systematically through the important points that you want to make in answer to the question. In doing this you will need to explain and define important concepts, outline the central theories that are relevant to the question you are trying to answer, and describe, briefly but informatively, the key pieces of evidence that support or undermine those theories. Remember: psychology is an empirical science. You always need to back up what you say with data from the research literature. Anecdote is no good – the plural of anecdote is not data!

In the main body you are developing an argument that should demonstrate to the reader why your conclusion is worth considering. A major weakness of many student essays is that they read like a 'laundry list' of theories and bits of data rather than a development of an argument. The basic idea is that you must try to develop your argument in an orderly fashion – point by point – so that it unfolds progressively and logically. You can do this by, for example, explicitly referring back to previous relevant material, moving the essay forward by asking questions and exemplifying key points.

Here's an annotated example to make this more concrete. It's in an essay on logical reasoning, specifically on the Wason selection task, a famous experiment that illustrates some of the frailties of human reasoning:

> The evidence presented so far shows that performance is poorer when the material in a logical reasoning task is abstract, but better when presented in a real-world context [*reference to*

back up material that has already been introduced and explained]. The question that now arises [*moves the essay forward*] is whether people's performance differs depending on the precise nature of the real-world context. For example, [*use of exemplification*] do people perform better on tasks that involve reasoning about moral issues or about prudential issues? [*use of question*].

Remember to include points of view that contrast with the argument that you are developing. You need to show that you have considered other important views on a question. Here's another concrete example – this time from an essay on learning – that illustrates this:

> It has been argued in the first section of this essay that the concept of operant conditioning provides a good way of understanding learning in rats. Tolman (1948), however, suggested that the phenomenon of latent learning casts doubt on the concept's usefulness. His main arguments will now be briefly examined and shown to be unconvincing. Latent learning is learning that. …

The main body of psychology essays will usually require:

- **Definition of key terms and concepts, especially those that are used in the essay question.**

- **Description of theories and how they purport to explain the phenomena relevant to the essay.**

- **Description of empirical studies.**

- **Analysis and evaluation of the extent to which empirical studies support or undermine theories.**

Your description of theories needs to concentrate on the key aspects, for example:

> Fodor (1983) defines a modular input system in terms of a cluster of ten properties. However, it is clear from Fodor (1985) that the key property is informational encapsulation. This property can be explained via an example …

Your discussion of relevant empirical studies should then concentrate on those that relate specifically to this aspect of the theory. You need to think carefully about exactly what you should include. You probably don't need to include full details of the design of an experiment, for example. Your main concern will usually be with the implications of the *findings* of an experiment or study. Here is an extended example:

> Marslen-Wilson and Tyler (1987) review evidence from a number of word-monitoring experiments and argue that they show pragmatic inferences occurring very early in the processing of the incoming speech stream, i.e. that pragmatic processing is fast. The basic idea of their experiments is to show that setting up an appropriate prior discourse context will

affect speed of recognition of a target word. They report, for instance, that the target word LEAD is monitored faster when it occurs in a sentence such as 'The lead was stripped off the roof', than in a sentence such as 'No lead puzzles some in the land of the text'; but it does so only when preceded by a sentence that sets up an appropriate discourse context such as 'The church was broken into last night'.

Why are these results relevant to Fodor's (1983) informational encapsulation hypothesis? On Fodor's picture the language module outputs, roughly, a representation of the literal meaning of a sentence. This means that the language module does not map a sentence onto discourse context – that is the job of the central systems. But if discourse context is processed by the central systems, then information about discourse context should not influence the processing of the language-input module, since the latter is *ex hypothesi* encapsulated from the former. Yet Marslen-Wilson and Tyler's results seem to show that discourse context does affect the operation of the language-input system in that it affects reaction times to target words in their monitoring experiments. The idea, with regard to the first example, is presumably, and intuitively, that if you've just read a sentence about churches being broken into, then a discourse context – that churches are often broken into and when they are they often have their lead roofs stolen – is constructed leading to lower RTs to the target word. So, it seems that Fodor either has to accept that language perception is unencapsulated or say that discourse context is computed by the language input module.

Use subheadings if it helps you to organise your thoughts and makes the essay clearer. Use paragraphs to separate main ideas or lines of argument. An important rule of thumb is: one sentence, one idea.

The conclusion

The conclusion must clearly and concisely state your answer to the question and should concisely remind the reader of the major reasons you have come to that conclusion. Go back to the title and check that you have done what it has asked. Have you analysed, compared and contrasted, evaluated, discussed and so on? You should also use the conclusion to remind the reader of the main steps in your argument.

A major weakness of many student essays is to fail to write a conclusion. Another is to write a conclusion that doesn't contain a clear statement of the view the student has formed on the topic of the essay.

Here is an extended annotated example of what a conclusion should be like:

Our aim has been to defend the legitimacy of Goldman's (1989) conception of the theory versus simulation debate as a debate between empirical theories pitched at a subpersonal level of description [*clear statement of the main aim of the essay*]. We have been concerned with the major problem that is posed for this cognitive-scientific conception of the debate by Heal's (1994) 'threat of collapse' argument. If she is right, then the cognitive-scientific simulation theory is nothing other than a version of the tacit-theory theory [*summary of conclusion of first phase of the essay*].

In Section 2, we set the difference of approach between Goldman and Heal within the more general framework of a two-by-two array of variations on the simulation theory. In Section 3, we identified the kinds of principles that belong in the minimal theoretical background for mental simulation. In Section 4, we explained the notion of tacit knowledge that Heal assumes. In Section 5, we began by acknowledging that Davies's earlier (1994) attempt to anticipate and respond to a version of the worry about collapse was inadequate [*reminders to the reader of the main stages of the argument*]. But, we rejected Heal's (1996) general argument for the claim that if a mechanism is used to simulate the operation of other mechanisms of the same kind, then it embodies tacit knowledge of theoretical principles about how mechanisms of that kind operate [*statement of one of the major conclusions reached on the way to achieving the overall aim of the essay*]. Heal is correct to maintain that prediction by mental simulation draws on psychological principles. But the principles do not go beyond those that have already been recognised as belonging in the minimal theoretical background for mental simulation [*summary of the reasons for that conclusion*]. So Heal's argument does not establish that Goldman's version of the simulation theory collapses into the theory theory [*brief statement of reasons why we have rejected Heal's argument*]. We ended by suggesting that it is not clear how, if Heal's argument had worked, her own version of the simulation theory would have avoided the same threat of collapse [*one sentence statement of the final point made in the essay*].

Some other points to note are detailed below.

Use of third person

It is a good idea to get used to writing in the third person (as some tutors don't like the use of 'I' and 'We'). For example:

> 'It can be shown …' instead of 'I have shown … '.
> 'The evidence presented above indicates that …' instead of 'I think that the evidence …'.
> 'It is useful to compare Fodor's view with …' instead of 'I have argued that …'.

Use of quotation

You can use quotations, but do so sparingly and only when you think it is absolutely justified, for example, when you want to show that someone really does hold the crazy view you are attributing to them. And, of course, don't forget to reference them! In general, you should see your job as to put the ideas of others into your own words so that your lecturers can see that you understand them.

Some style issues

You should also avoid rhetorical flourishes/excesses. For example:

> With an experiment that can only be described as breathtaking, the eminent psychologist swept away all opposition and demonstrated to all those willing to listen that….

Remember that you are writing formal prose, not writing an email, text message, letter or article in the 'soaraway Sun'.

Don't try to be funny – it really never works.

Don't be abusive or dismissive, for example, say something is 'rubbish' – you are apprentices, not authorities (and even the greatest authorities will not, generally, be abusive – at least not in print).

Drafting and redrafting

It is unlikely that you will be happy with your first version and it is important that you *reflect* (the last component of OCR) on what you have written. You need to try to develop the skill of putting yourself in the position of the marker. Try to identify the questions that the marker is likely to be asking at the end of each paragraph. If you have written the essay well, then the paragraph should address those questions.

It *can* be useful to swap essays with another student and to give constructive criticism of one another's work. For instance, if you have failed to explain something, then another student (especially if they are not doing psychology) may spot this. But you need to be prepared to be honest with one another and not just reassuring. However, you need to take *great* care if you do this, for two reasons. One is that you need to trust that the other student won't copy chunks of your text because then you could *both* be charged with plagiarism. The other reason is that you could be at risk of accidental plagiarism, where one of you might copy the structure of the others essay. We discuss plagiarism in detail later in the chapter, but the concern here is that one student might adopt the same essay structure as you (or vice versa) and simply rephrase the material you present. Remember, this is unacceptable.

Another useful tip is to read your essay out loud to yourself or to someone else. This is a good way of spotting unclear writing and poor English.

Self-assessment

You need to be able to develop your skills in essay writing to the point where you can assess accurately the quality of your own work. If you have no idea about whether your work is of a particular standard, then you are failing to understand what is required of you. But this is a hard skill to develop. One piece of information that will help you is your department's published marking criteria; these should give you some idea of the standard you need to reach in order to gain a particular classification. You should be aware also that what is expected of you changes as you progress through the course. At level 1, tutors are interested in checking that you have understood basic concepts, key theories and a range of often classic studies that are relevant to these theories. They will also be interested to check that you have begun to develop the rudiments of how to structure your essays in the right way, and have started to engage in the process of critically evaluating the material you discuss. While you will be encouraged to begin using the research literature, it will not be expected that you can deploy this extensively in your writing. Mastery of textbook material is expected. At level 2 you will be expected to consolidate your knowledge and essay-writing skills, but you will now not achieve high marks just by careful reportage of material from textbooks. Tutors will now be more interested in whether you can develop your own 'take' on the material, and will be looking for your ability to compare and contrast different approaches and theories. At level 3 it is expected that the basics of essay writing have been mastered. High marks will now only be achieved if your command of the material is secure and if your essays contain rigorous argumentation and provide a clear and concise answer to the question you have decided to tackle. Reliance on textbook material alone will be inadequate, and you should be able to incorporate into your answer material that you have culled from the research literature.

But, developing this skill requires that you be honest with yourself and that you reflect on questions such as:

'Have I really understood why the experiment I have cited is important for the theory I am discussing?'

'Have I really explained the essential features of the psychological model I am evaluating?'

'Have I actually gone on to evaluate the model?'

'Have I given a clear answer to the question I have attempted?'

It is important that you take responsibility for what you write. Answering these kinds of questions enables you to do that. You should have a reason for saying everything that you say. This actually applies to each individual paragraph and sentence of your essay! For each paragraph and sentence that you write: do you know what purpose it serves in the overall development of your argument? If you have no answer to this question, then why have you written what you have written?

Writing is an exacting and demanding discipline. You must avoid the trap of thinking that writing is a simple matter of transcribing your thoughts onto paper. It is – as we hope to have demonstrated – a much more creative and interesting exercise than that.

Using Feedback From Coursework

The most helpful information to guide your development should be the feedback you receive from tutors on work you submit. You will generally always get written feedback as well as a mark for your coursework essays. Lecturers spend a good deal of time on this, so it is worthwhile spending some time reading it and thinking about it. Remember also that lecturers usually have office hours when you can see them to discuss their feedback. You should take advantage of this when it is available. In general, for each piece of marked work make sure that you have a good idea of why you received the mark you did, of the strengths and weaknesses of your work and of how you can improve in future. If you do not, then you are wasting the feedback and must make an appointment with the appropriate member of staff so that you do understand the mark you received.

Practical Reports

In the course of your psychology degree, you will almost certainly write a number of practical reports. Students are often wary of practical reports as there are very specific requirements for the way they should be written; but this is really to your advantage as it means that reports are very straightforward, once you have understood what you need to do. It's important once again to be aware of what the marker is looking for in your report. First, they want to see that you have structured the report correctly. If you haven't even done that, you are likely to be seen as a weaker student. Second, the marker wants to see a short report that is clear in all parts and, as a result, very easy to mark. Finally, the marker wants to see a comprehensive report that provides all and only the necessary information within the word limit.

We don't have the space to include examples of good practical reports, but you can obtain examples yourself very easily as the practical report is essentially a shortened form of a journal article where a study has been reported. Therefore, to find examples of good reports, simply read what authors have written in peer-reviewed journals (for example, any journal published by the American Psychological Association). For specific topic areas, why not ask your tutor to recommend some good examples.

There are some common errors that we have found students make when completing reports, so we highlight these for each section of the report. However, it is also important to make sure that the overall presentation of the report is appropriate. For example, text should usually be black, 12-point Times New Roman or something similar with only bold, underline or italics used. Text should usually be at least one-and-a-half or double-line spaced. We have had reports in smaller fonts and they are very hard to read, and it makes the marker feel old, and we have also had reports in larger fonts, which make the marker feel that you think they are old! Try to save resources by starting a new page only when necessary. It wastes paper to have one page for the one sentence for the title, for example. Including redundant material also bulks up the report, which makes the pile of reports heavy to carry, and when faced with a lot of work the marker won't be delighted by a large document as that will take longer to mark (and, if anything, suggests that the writer hasn't focussed on the key issues).

Writing a good report is a skill; it is one that requires practice and thought, but can be learned. The simplest way to think about a report is that it contains the following components:

- **Title**

- **Abstract**

- **Introduction**

- **Method**

- **Results**

- **Discussion**

- **References**

- **Appendix.**

In the pages that follow, we consider each of these in turn and give examples of good and bad practice. We hope these will help you, but don't despair if your first, or even second, attempt isn't too successful. Remember, it's a skill, like riding a bicycle, and some learn the skill faster than others.

Title

It should be really easy to write a title, but it actually does take practice. It's tempting to simply use 'Practical report', but that is uninformative as it reveals nothing about the specific topic of the report. In the title you should identify manipulations and measures, that is, the independent variables that you manipulated or were interested in (like gender) and what you measured – the dependent variable(s). Imagine that you have carried out a study that has involved observing whether there are differences in the ways in which men and women avoid colliding into one another on the street. Entitling your report 'Collision study' doesn't tell us enough about this particular study. We want to know more: collisions of what or whom? A better title would be 'Gender differences in observed collision avoidance behaviour in pedestrians' as it tells us a reasonable amount about the study. The title tells us that the study is going to focus on gender differences, so it's going to be looking at how gender – whether someone is male or female – appears to affect their behaviour. In fact, we know more than that as the title tells us that it is about pedestrian behaviour. So we can see that this study will be looking at different behaviour in pedestrians for men and women when they avoid collisions. Note that we don't know everything about the study, but we do have a reasonable idea of the focus. We would know enough to decide if we were interested by reading the abstract, where we would expect to find more detail.

However, it's also worth noting that too much information can be a bad thing too. We hope you can see why the following is *not* a good title: 'Gender differences in collision avoidance behaviour in pedestrians who were not carrying bags or accompanied by children and who were observed on a Tuesday afternoon on the main shopping street in Leeds in December 2006.'

Make sure that you don't include any unnecessary words such as 'An experiment to study ...'. A good way of deciding if words are unnecessary is to ask yourself whether you could use those words for any practical or whether they are specific to the particular study you are writing up.

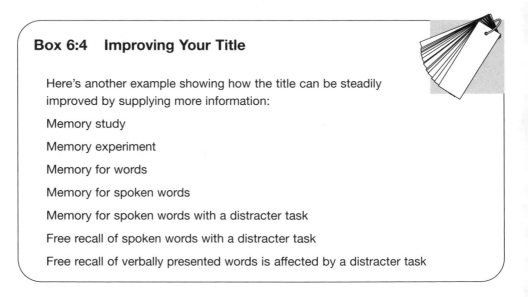

Box 6:4 Improving Your Title

Here's another example showing how the title can be steadily improved by supplying more information:

Memory study

Memory experiment

Memory for words

Memory for spoken words

Memory for spoken words with a distracter task

Free recall of spoken words with a distracter task

Free recall of verbally presented words is affected by a distracter task

Abstract

The Abstract comes straight after the title, but is usually written last as it is a summary of the whole report. One of the best ways of producing an abstract is to summarise those four report sections that we highlighted earlier: Introduction, Method, Results and Discussion. After all, the reader wants to know:

- *Why* you did what you did.

- *What* you did.

- **What you *found*.**

- **What it all *means*!**

So, if you write a sentence or two on each of these, you should have produced a reasonable abstract. However, the abstract should rarely exceed 100 words, so make sure you keep things short and to the point. Remember, the detail is in the report itself and the abstract is simply the summary. Where students tend to go wrong here is very similar to where they go wrong with the title: either too much or too little information.

The funniest abstract we have read was one that went like this: 'In this report I will provide an overview of an area of psychology, highlighting a particular issue and identifying an hypothesis. Then I will describe the method used to collect the data. I will then summarise the results. Finally, I will discuss the results and consider their implications.' This abstract made us laugh because it is a good description of what you try to do in an abstract, but tells you *absolutely nothing* about that particular study. Instead, each of those sentences needs to be fleshed out with detail.

For example, you need to begin by stating the background to your study. Note that you are not *discussing* previous research here; you can simply say 'The X model of memory predicts that …'. If you write a sentence like that, you may worry that there isn't sufficient detail to understand what the X model is or to understand the prediction. That's OK as you will expand on that in the Introduction. Now, let's consider the 'method used to collect the data'. We'd write something like 'Participants indicated whether they had seen a word or non-word using a button box' or 'Participants had to adjust the orientation of a bar in front of them to match the orientation of a line on a computer display'. Note that even though we haven't told you anything else about these experiments, you already have an idea of what the participants actually did. It's similar for the Results section, where you should keep things simple. For example, 'Participants were faster to respond to words than non-words, but showed more errors for the former compared to the latter.' It's not usually necessary to include statistical detail in the abstract, but focus on simply stating what you found. You just want to indicate the main finding. For example, you would say that there was or was not a difference between the experimental and control condition. If things were more complicated than that, you can say a few words in the concluding sentence. Otherwise, the concluding sentence should give the reader an idea of the implications of your results. For example, 'The findings cast doubt on the X model of memory and they are more inconsistent with the Y model of memory.'

You might be asked to produce what's called a 'structured' Abstract, which has the subheadings: objectives, design, methods, results and conclusions. Below we have given an indication of what is required in each section. Structured abstracts are popular for conferences where abstracts are used to decide if the writer can give an oral or poster presentation as the subheadings force the writer to focus on key issues (or reveal their confusion). You might find it useful to write your abstract as a structured abstract and then convert it into a non-structured abstract.

Objectives: State the primary objective of the report and the major hypothesis tested (if appropriate).

Design: Describe the design of the study and describe the principal reasoning for the procedures adopted.

Methods: State the procedures used, including the selection and number of participants, the interventions or experimental manipulations, and the primary outcome measures.

Results: State the main results of the study. Numerical data may be included, but should be kept to a minimum.

Conclusions: State the conclusions that can be drawn from the data provided.

Introduction

The Introduction is probably the section where we have found that students most often put in a great deal of work, but don't produce what is actually required for a report. For the Introduction, it is very tempting to write a mini-essay showing a great deal of knowledge about the general topic area of the practical, but then find yourself forced to squeeze in the other sections of the report, either because you are running out of time or are in danger of going beyond your word limit. If you do this, the likely result will be a low mark, as the Introduction should be a specific introduction to the *particular* study that you performed. So, you should focus on the issues that directly relate to your study rather than provide a general overview of the area. In particular, you should identify the key theory or theories that are relevant to the study you performed and make it clear that you understand them. It is also important that you include explicit references here to published work, for example, book chapters and journal articles. Sometimes students can see referencing an idea as a sign of weakness. You might feel that you should have had the ideas or insights, but it is important to recognise that you are expected to build upon the work of others, and it is more impressive to see that a student has found relevant information than for the student to claim that it is all their own work.

Finally, the section should finish with the experimental hypothesis(es), and it should be clear how these hypotheses have emerged from the theories you have discussed At undergraduate level, it is unusual to state the null hypothesis as well as the experimental hypothesis (you won't ever see the null hypothesis stated in a peer-reviewed journal article). However, for your first few practical reports your tutor might require that you state the null hypothesis, so see your own guidelines for the practical report.

Method

The most important aim of this section is to provide sufficient information to allow someone else to replicate your study. The Method section has three subheadings to help make it clear exactly what you did, with whom and using what. We have been surprised by how often students fail to use those subheadings. It's a shame, as subheadings help to structure the information and actually makes writing this section easier. It is also very useful, as with essays, to ask someone else to read through this section so that they can spot where you may have mentally filled in the gaps and not been as explicit as you need to be in the text. You need to use the past tense throughout, indicating what *was* done, rather than giving a 'recipe'. Also, resist the temptation to use bullet points. You need to write in sentences for all the sections of a practical report, including the Method section.

Method subheading – participants
You don't want to describe every one of your participants, but you should indicate how they were recruited and what characteristics matter depending on the hypothesis or research question that you are investigating. If you went to your local antenatal class to recruit women who were pregnant for the first time, then you need to make that clear here, for example, 'Participants were recruited using a poster that asked women who were pregnant for the first time to volunteer for a test of intelligence.' In addition, it is usual to indicate relevant information such as gender and age range. However, you need to think a little. If you stated for this *pregnancy* study that 'The 34 participants were female', then you aren't exactly displaying your intelligence! Another common mistake here is to write something like 'The 24 participants were half male and half female.' The reader knows what you mean, or thinks they do, but it's lazy use of the English language and again doesn't show you at your best. (It could mean that each person was half male and half female!)

Method subheading – apparatus or stimuli
You need to state whether you used apparatus or stimuli or both. The former refers to equipment like computers and button boxes, whereas the latter refers to pictures, sounds, smells, tastes and so on. Students often find it difficult when they start writing reports to work out exactly what information is needed. The essential idea, remember, is to give information about the specific things that are needed to enable a replication of the study. So, you don't need to give details of the furniture (it is assumed that someone at a computer is sitting on a chair, for example), *unless* the furniture is part of the experimental manipulation. An example where you would need to mention the furniture would be if you were comparing the effects of different sorts of chairs on performance using a computer. Similarly, you would not normally state here that participants used a pen and paper for making responses (although you might in the next section).

Method subheading – procedure

It is particularly important to provide a precise description of the procedures that you used to collect your data, because otherwise it is difficult to interpret the results. Therefore, you should also include details of the design of the study as well as the exact procedures that were used. For example, it is important to make clear which is the experimental condition and which is the control condition, if you have one. Again, you are aiming to provide enough information so that someone can understand what you did and replicate your study. However, it is also important to ensure that you don't include unnecessary information, so carefully read through what you have written with that in mind.

It is good practice to write the procedure *before* you collect your data. Otherwise, you may discover that you didn't worry about some aspect of the procedure when you collected the data (say, the instructions that you gave each participant) and then realise that this omission could have greatly affected your results. If your procedure involved the use of written instructions or a questionnaire that you produced, you should include that material in the Appendix to facilitate replication and also interpretation of your results.

Results

Here you should simply present your results, including any analysis of your data. You should not include your raw data here. You might, however, be asked by your tutor to include raw data in the Appendix (to enable the tutor to check that you have carried out the study, but more importantly to enable them to work out what you have done if your results or analysis aren't correct). This section needs to *summarise* the results of your study so normally includes explanatory text and figures and/or tables. It is important that you put into words the main 'message' of your figures and/or tables. It is not that different from when your lecturers put up a slide with data and takes the time to highlight what you should be looking at so that you understand that slide.

Text

The text should be brief, but should *describe* the results comprehensively. You are trying to help an intelligent reader to understand your results. However, take care not to *discuss* the results. As you might guess, discussion comes in the next section – the Discussion. A good strategy for writing the results section is to describe the important findings first in words and then introduce the numerical and graphical evidence for support.

Figures and tables

Figures and tables should be self-contained and self-explanatory, which means that they always need a title and might even need some supplementary text to explain what they reveal. You should check with you tutor to see if they want supplementary text. The tables must be numbered consecutively (Table 1, Table 2, and so on) and any figures are numbered in a separate sequence (Figure 1, Figure 2, and so on). By convention, titles are written above tables, but below figures. Do not present the data in more than one form. If the data are included in a table, do not present them again in the text unless some *new relationship* is being highlighted. Remember at all times that figures and tables are used to *communicate* information to the reader *clearly* and *concisely*. Titles and labels are essential and if you include diagrams, use them by explaining them in the text. Always ask yourself if the diagrams add to what you are trying to say and make sure you understand what your diagrams mean.

How do I produce a good table?

You should keep things as simple as possible with a clear, informative title and proper labelling. It's the convention not to use vertical lines in a table. Here's an example:

Table 1   Mean and standard deviations of eye contact in a two-minute period for the control and experimental conditions

	Mean	Standard Deviation
Control (no alcohol)	8.3	2.2
Experimental (alcohol)	6.2	1.8

How do I produce a good figure?

You should ensure that both axes are properly labelled (giving units of measurement where appropriate). If symbols are used, then ensure that you have a key that clearly identifies them.

At undergraduate level, you are likely to produce only four different types of figures in the results. You may also produce figures in the Introduction to display better the ideas behind a theory.

The four kinds of figures are:

- **bar charts**

- **histograms**

- **line graphs**

- **scatterplot.**

Barcharts and *histograms* are very similar, but there are subtle differences. Bar charts have gaps between the bars, whereas histograms have their bars right next to each other. Bar charts are normally used where we have categorical data, such as hair colour (for example, brunette, blonde, black), where there isn't a clear ordering to the data. On the other hand, histograms represent different points on a numerical measurement scale (for example, school years).

For both bar charts and histograms there are some simple guidelines:

- **Your aim is to show frequencies (for example, percentage of males in a sample).**

- **Keep number of categories low (don't have more than half a dozen separate bars).**

- **Keep 'combined' categories meaningful (for example, for occupations collapse different jobs into 'manual workers' and 'office workers').**

- **Report frequencies as totals (simple frequencies) or as percentage frequencies.**

Line graphs are actually histograms without the bars but joining the tops of the bars with a straight line. They are good for highlighting trends in data and especially good if you have more than one factor under consideration as you can have different lines that overlap but are still clear.

Scatterplots are used to examine the relationship between two different variables that are non-categorical.

Let's look at some examples that we've produced using MS Excel, which is a popular package that can be used to produce graphs. You can, of course, use the graphical abilities of any other statistical package (for example, SPSS).

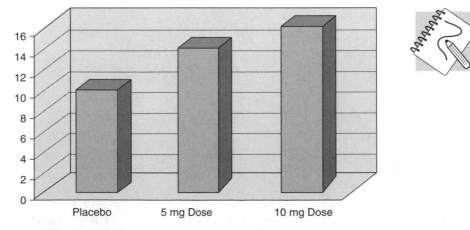

Figure 1   Experiment

You might think this bar chart is fine, but there are a number of problems: the title is pretty useless, there is no labelling of the y-axis (vertical) or the x-axis (horizontal), the 3-D effect is distracting (and can be misleading) and the background is fussy with too much detail.

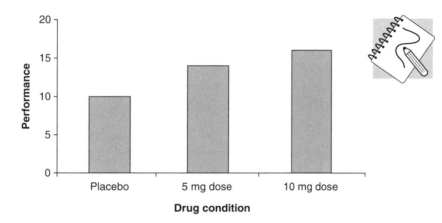

Figure 2   The effect of Drug X on performance

Note how the graph is so much clearer now without all the clutter seen in the first version.

Let's look at another example.

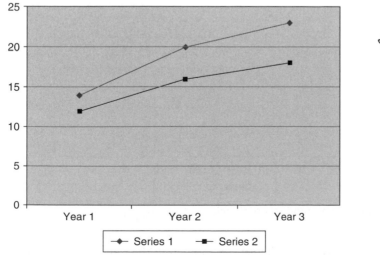

Figure 3

No problems with 3-D effects this time, but it's hard to see the lines against the background and the lines are not really labelled at all. What is meant by 'Series 1' and 'Series 2'?

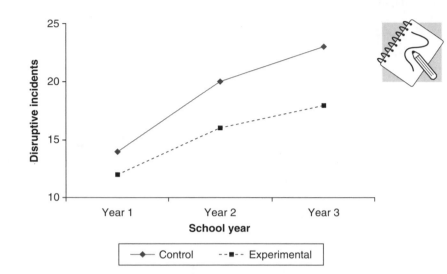

Figure 4   Frequency of observed disruptive incidents for students

Much better. The scale for the vertical axis has been changed so that you can see more easily the difference between the two conditions (which are now clearly labelled and more visible).

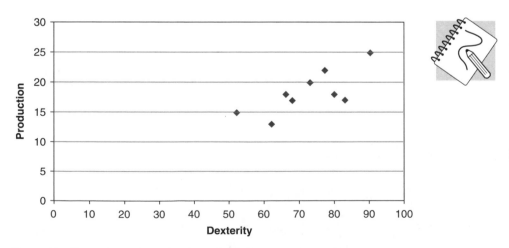

Figure 5   Dexterity and production of units

The big problem here is that the data are hidden in the top corner and the data points are small and difficult to see.

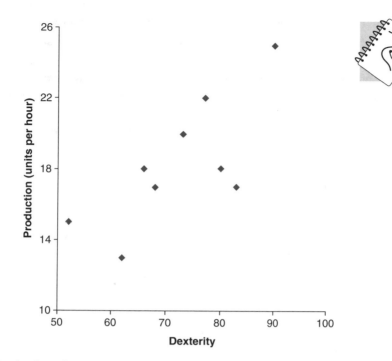

Figure 6   Production of units related to dexterity

We have made a number of changes here. The points are easier to see and the horizontal grid lines have been removed because they don't help us see the pattern in our results. In addition, we have changed the shape of the graph so that it is almost square, making it is easier to see the underlying relationship that can be obscured when the graph is stretched along one variable or another.

Finally, the Results section is the part of the report that seems to cause students the biggest problems. There are a number of common errors, some of which we have already mentioned but it's worth collecting them together so that you can check through these for every report. They include:

- **Forgetting to include any text at all! You need text to describe what the results actually show.**

- **Forgetting to include the results of any statistical tests, when these have been calculated. You need to include these to demonstrate that sufficient evidence has been found in your data to indicate that differences have been found between conditions.**

- **Duplicating material in tables _and_ figures. You need to present your data in one form only.**

- **Using the word 'prove'. As we explained in Chapter 4, we never 'prove' anything in science, but we may find evidence to support our hypothesis.**

- **For figures, the most common errors are to make them too small and to forget to label them (and that includes the title). The latter is also true of tables.**

- **Finally, don't 'borrow' someone else's figure. That is plagiarism and it's surprisingly easy for a marker to spot!**

Discussion

In this section, you need to discuss, interpret and draw conclusions from your results. Importantly, you need to do so in relation to your statement of the problem at the end of the Introduction. In essence, you are telling the reader what your results mean. You do not present new results here, nor do you repeat the results (what we call 'redescription' of the data). One of the most common errors found when students start producing reports is to begin the Discussion section by restating the results, so make sure that you resist that temptation.

Finally, you should highlight how the procedure that you used might have affected the results you obtained and in particular you should suggest how the experiment might be improved by outlining further experiments that could resolve any outstanding issues. Student practicals are sometimes designed to have one or more design limitations and it's important to identify those problems, explain why they are a problem and suggest how they can be avoided in a future study. If your results don't agree with the existing literature, it is important that you comment on why that might be the case. This section is your opportunity to display critical thinking and since it's the last section, it is most likely to have the greatest effect on determining the mark you are awarded. And do make sure that you don't finish with something like 'I think these results are a good basis on which we can build to increase our understanding of the human mind.' Rather than sounding impressive, it just reads as empty, glib words.

References

It is important that you do not include material that you haven't read or haven't cited in the text. Further information on referencing is given later in the chapter.

Appendix

The Appendix is not a rubbish bin! There is a temptation to include anything and everything that just might be relevant. However, if you include unnecessary information, you will be penalised as it suggests that you don't understand what is important and what is not. If an Appendix is required, it should contain items such as:

- **A questionnaire that *you* created, but *not* a 'standard' questionnaire.**

- **Example stimuli such as a line drawing to illustrate the level of detail in a picture.**

Examples of inappropriate materials that students sometimes include are:

- **Copies of tutor handouts.**

- **Figures or tables showing the results; these should be in the Results section.**

- **Raw data (unless specifically requested).**

- **Copies of calculations or statistical output (unless specifically requested).**

- **Completed questionnaires (unless specifically requested).**

Using feedback on your practical report

It is very tempting to ignore feedback when you get your work back. Some students only seem to care that they got a pass mark and don't think it's worth looking at the feedback since if they have passed, they won't be doing that assessment again. However, ignoring the feedback is a bad mistake.

The structure of the practical report means that it is likely that the feedback from the tutor will reflect the report's structure. So the tutor is likely to indicate that a particular section wasn't as good or was much better compared to the rest of the report.

Referencing

You might think that it's strange to have a long discussion on referencing. After all, don't references come at the end of a piece of work and isn't it all pretty simple? Both of those statements are true, but referencing properly is essential, both so you can demonstrate the background reading that you have done in producing an assessment and also to ensure that you don't pass off someone else's work as your own and commit the offence of plagiarism.

With the possibilities offered by the Internet and increasing pressures on students, plagiarism has become an important issue. Plagiarism is greatly facilitated by the use of computers linked to the Internet where cut-and-paste of relevant material and online essay-writing services are readily available. However, academics are greatly concerned by the possibility that students could cheat to get a degree, so various strategies are in place to detect plagiarism. We are not going to tell you about all of them, but one in particular is worth highlighting. If you go to www.submit.ac.uk, you will find 'The JISC plagiarism detection service' which 'enables institutions and staff to carry out electronic comparison of students' work against electronic sources including other students' work.' If student work is uploaded onto the service, it can be checked against material available on the Internet, other student work submitted at the same time (or in an archive) and even textbooks! The system is not perfect, but the penalties for using work without attribution are severe at university level. Those penalties include expulsion in extreme cases and that could finish your career before it has started. After all, if you have had to leave your course because you cheated (and that's what plagiarism is), then why would another course want you?

We have already discussed how to obtain material for assessments in Chapter 5 'Teaching Situations' and will expand on that in Chapter 7 'Using Resources Effectively'. In situations where you are taking notes that you might use later for an assessment, it is essential that you make clear where your material was obtained. If your notes are identical to a section of text, you should put that text in quotation marks or use a particular colour of highlighter pen to indicate to yourself that you mustn't use that text in that form unless it is clear that it is a quotation that you have properly attributed.

Quotations

'The strength of women comes from the fact that psychology cannot explain us. Men can be analysed, women . . . merely adored.' Oscar Wilde, *An Ideal Husband*

Quotations can be very effective in written and oral presentations, but they should be seen as a powerful spice: a little can be very effective, but a lot spoils the dish. In your work, you should avoid routine quotation of sources. A student who uses too many quotations is demonstrating that they lack the ability to take their identified source material, understand it and present it in their own words. After all, if the assessment is very straightforward you could find a perfect answer on the Internet. Would you expect to receive a first class mark if you put quotation marks around a whole essay produced that way?!

It can be difficult to take original sources and rephrase them in your own words; it's particularly difficult if English is not your first language. One technique is to ensure that you understand the material in a particular paragraph and then try to write it down without looking at the text. Another useful technique is to have a number of different sources as you will then find that you want to make a different argument to the first source that you read as there may be other studies or theories that you wish to highlight. Remember that your tutors don't expect you to develop brand new psychological theories, but what they do expect of you is that you can understand existing theories and present evidence that supports those theories as well as evidence that is problematic for those theories and provides support for competing theories. Referencing properly also allows you to gain credit for your background reading.

Plagiarism

It can be difficult to give strict rules on where to draw the line when it comes to plagiarism. Try the following exercise.

Box 6:5   Plagiarism

1. Copying a paragraph word-for-word from a source without acknowledgement.

2. Copying a paragraph and making small changes, for example, replacing two verbs with different verbs, replacing an adjective with a similar adjective. Listing the original source in the list of references.

3. Constructing a paragraph by using sentences from the original but omitting one or two and putting one or two in a different order. There is an in-text acknowledgement at the end, for example, (Jones, 1999) plus the original source is included in the reference list.

4. Composing a paragraph by taking short phrases of 10 to 15 words from a number of sources and putting them together, adding words of your own to make a coherent paragraph; including all the original sources in the reference list.

5. Writing a paragraph based on something you have read with the points in a different order. The new version will also have changes in the amount of detail used and the examples cited; including an in-text acknowledgement, for example (Jones, 1999), and listing the original source in the reference list.

6. Quoting a paragraph by placing it in block format with the source cited in the text and list of references.

Number 1 is plagiarism, but number 6 is not. Where did you draw the line?

Created by Jude Carroll, based on an exercise in *Academic Writing for Graduate Students* by Swales and Feak, University of Michigan, 1993.

Students who are caught plagiarising give last-minute panic and misunderstanding the rules as reasons for their cheating. You can avoid the first by being organised and the second by ensuring that you take great care in following your department's rules.

When does collaborating become collusion?

It is very useful to work together with another student for a number of reasons. You can share your ideas and discover any gaps or misunderstandings that either of you have. It is also a good way to find out how someone else is obtaining relevant materials, either from another university library or a very good website. However, that collaboration can become collusion if you work together too closely. For example, if you both worked together on a report, the marker might feel that all the sections are too similar and you could risk an investigation for plagiarism. The best strategy is to 'collaborate by talking and not by writing'. It is good to share ideas, but the closer your collaboration is to the assessment the more likely it is that your assessed work will share the same order of material and even use the same phrasing.

How to reference

There are different reference styles that are used in psychology. However, the style that is used most in psychology is set out in the *Publication Manual of the American Psychological Association* published, unsurprisingly, by the American Psychological Association. It isn't really worth buying the manual unless you intend going into academia, but you might like to look at a copy in your library to see how to reference over 70 different types of sources! Fortunately, most of the material you will cite in your assessments will be books (including collections of essays) and journal articles.

Why should I be careful citing material from the Internet?

The Internet is an incredibly powerful tool, which makes available many libraries-worth of material of psychology at your desk, so why should you be careful about citing that material in your assessments? It's important to remember that one of the strengths of the Internet is also a weakness – anyone can put up material. If you think about the sources that we use in psychology for peer-reviewed journal articles, they are mainly peer-reviewed journal articles and books. Both are subject to an editorial process and the publishers jealously guard their reputations to ensure that any material they publish is of high quality. In addition, once something is published, it becomes is a fixed document that will not change. A book can be published in a different edition, but the previous editions still exist and can be cited. Unfortunately, webpages do not necessarily have an editorial process and those pages are not unchanging, so citing them is problematic.

Referencing in the text

Citing references in your assessment is actually quite easy as you should give the author's name (just the surname) followed by the date of publication. If there is more than one author, you should give all the names. If the name forms part of a sentence the date is enclosed in parentheses so you have 'Freeman and Stone (2005) claimed that ...'. Alternatively, both the name and date can be enclosed in parentheses and separated by a comma so you could have 'It has been claimed (Freeman and Stone, 2005) that ...'. It's better to use the first of these two alternatives as the text reads more easily, but both are acceptable. Some courses may also require you to give page references as well, so give the page number of the relevant page as 'Freeman and Stone (2005, p. 28)' or '(Freeman and Stone, 2005, p. 28)' as appropriate. If you have used a secondary source (for example, you read about a study in a textbook), you should make that clear in the text. For example, 'Dockrell (1990, cited in Stone, 1995) found that ...' with Stone (1995) in your list of references. However, do try to read original texts as they contain more information and you might disagree with the interpretation made by the person who reported the original study. Another reason to avoid using secondary sources is that it looks unambitious to the marker if you have only read textbooks rather than trying to get to grips with the original work.

If you need to cite again the same reference in the same assessment and there are more than two authors, you can abbreviate what might be a long list to the first author's surname plus '*et al.*' followed by the date. So you might cite Stone, Freeman and Joiner (2004) for the first time, and Stone *et al.* (2004) for further citations.

Do not cite things that have been said by your lecturer or tutor in lectures or seminars. If the tutor has mentioned something relevant to your assessment, you should identify the original source of that information. For example, the lecturer might refer to the Pandemonium Model and if they haven't given you explicit references, you would have to find out about the person who came up with the idea. In this case, you would discover that Oliver Selfridge developed the model in 1959 and it was modified by Lindsay and Norman in 1972. Then, in your text you might refer to 'The Pandemonium Model was originally developed by Selfridge (1959) and later modified by Lindsay and Norman (1972) into a bottom-up theory of pattern recognition.' If you can't find a reference, don't be afraid to ask the lecturer as you may have misheard or misspelled the crucial words. Do avoid writing vague references such as 'Most psychologists now accept that ...' as it's asking for trouble. Similarly, avoid saying 'It is commonly known that ...' as sometimes what is commonly known isn't true. Instead, you should find an appropriate reference. For changes in the way people live, a good source is government reports (such as the Department of Health – www.dh.gov.uk) that range from how much alcohol people drink to how much they weigh.

Reference section

At the end of your assessment, you need to have a References section. Unlike some of the other subjects, psychology does *not* use a 'bibliography', which is a list of sources that you have read in producing your work. Your References should list all those sources that you have cited in the text and you must *not* include any material that is not cited in the text.

Below, we have given you some examples of the references that you will need to include. All the examples contain three essential elements of information:

1 *Author*: all authors of the work, with surnames and initials in inverted order, for example, Freeman, R.P.J. rather than R.P.J. Freeman.

2 *Title*: of the article, chapter or book (underlined *or* in italics).

3 *Facts of publication*: different for journals, books and chapters in edited books.

Finally, note that despite providing lots of examples and explanations, we are amazed at how often a piece of work is let down by poor or non-existent referencing.

Book
Dockrell, J. E. & McShane, J. (1993). *Children's Learning Difficulties: A Cognitive Approach.* London: Blackwell.

Collection of essays, readings etc.
Davies, M. & Stone, A. (Eds.). (1995). *Mental Simulation.* Oxford: Blackwell.

Chapter in edited book
Booth, D. A., Gibson, E. L., Toase, A. M. & Freeman, R.P.J. (1994). Small objects of desire: the recognition of appropriate foods and drinks and its neural mechanisms. In C. R. Legg & D. A. Booth (Eds.), *Appetite: Neural and Behavioural Bases* (pp. 98–126). Oxford: OUP.

Journal article
Gough, B. & Reavey, P. (1997). Parental accounts regarding the physical punishment of children: Discourses of dis/empowerment. *Child Abuse & Neglect, 21*(5), 417–30.

Poster session
Gold, L. M. (1998). *Temporal integration in vision.* Paper presented at the meeting of the European Society for Cognitive Psychology. Jerusalem, Israel.

Book with corporate author as publisher
American Psychological Association. (1994). *Publication Manual of the American Psychological Association* (4th ed.).

On-line journal article
Thomas, M. & Stone, A. (1998, June). Connectionism is a progressive research programme. *Psycoloquy* [On-line serial], *9* (36). Available http://www.cogsci.soton.ac.uk/
psyc-bin/newpsy?9.36

Other Forms of Assessment

Essays and practical reports are the most common forms of assessment used in psychology departments. But you may, from time to time, be faced with other types of
assessment task. We will briefly review some of these.

Short-answer examinations

These kinds of examination are often used in introductory courses when the lecturer
wants to ensure that you have understood some basic facts and data. All of the points
made above about communication apply to short answers. They should also be structured. In the main, the best way to approach this task is by aiming to provide one sub-
part of the main body of an essay.

Multiple-choice examinations

These are very different animals from the assessment tasks we have discussed up to
now. They are, again, used to test basic factual knowledge, including knowledge of
research methods and statistics where there are definite right and wrong answers. As
with all exams, make sure you know exactly what is required. For instance, do you lose
points for wrong answers? If so, then avoid guessing.

Oral presentations

You may have to give a brief oral presentation in a seminar and most students are ter-
rified of having to do this. It can be quite frightening when you first have to address a
group, but it does get easier with experience. Particularly for the first few times you do
this, you may want to produce a complete script of exactly what you are going to say
and even include directions to yourself such as 'put overhead on projector'. However,
if you choose this method, do make sure that you practise in front of friends and, in particular, try to get the speed right so that you keep to your time limit and try to speak as
naturally as you can, keeping to your normal rhythm – in other words, try not to drone!
Normally, oral presentations would be a maximum of 15 minutes, so you can only cover
a small number of ideas in that time. As a rule of thumb: one slide, one idea. Another
rule of thumb is to allow two minutes maximum for each slide.

If you are using overheads (which is a good idea as they can literally help to illustrate a point), make sure they are uncluttered and take the time to talk through them so that your audience can understand them. A common mistake when using overheads is to talk to the screen and not the audience – try to avoid this.

Finally, don't worry about being nervous. Everyone is nervous giving a public presentation (even if they don't show it) and the audience is usually on your side.

Posters

You might be asked to produce a poster for an assessment. A poster is usually a presentation of experimental work that is literally posted onto a board or wall for people to read. The easiest way to design a poster is to follow the section headings we gave for the practical report earlier in this chapter. You might allow one side of A4 for each of the Introduction, Methods, Results and Discussion, not forgetting any tables or graphs and References. Thus, a poster will usually run to no more than six or seven pages of A4. Depending on the instructions you are given, you might want to enlarge these and to laminate them.

The main point to remember is that people have to stand and read the poster. It is a good idea, therefore, to avoid excessive blocks of text. Break the text up with boxes, bullet points and diagrams, for example. Also make sure you use a large enough font for people to read with ease.

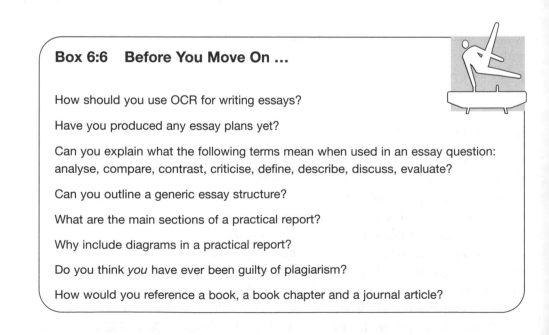

Box 6:6   Before You Move On …

How should you use OCR for writing essays?

Have you produced any essay plans yet?

Can you explain what the following terms mean when used in an essay question: analyse, compare, contrast, criticise, define, describe, discuss, evaluate?

Can you outline a generic essay structure?

What are the main sections of a practical report?

Why include diagrams in a practical report?

Do you think *you* have ever been guilty of plagiarism?

How would you reference a book, a book chapter and a journal article?

7 Using Resources Effectively

LEARNING OUTCOMES

1. To be aware of the resources available in a psychology laboratory.
2. To be aware of the range of computer software you will have available.
3. To understand the value of psychology societies both in your department and nationally.
4. To be aware of the resources in a university library.
5. To understand the importance of journals as well as books.
6. To be aware of the electronic databases available for psychology students.

Introduction

To succeed in your psychology degree, it is important to understand and be able to use the huge range of resources available to you. Academics in psychology were some of the first to eagerly embrace the Internet, and as a result there is much psychological material available to the browser who knows where to look. However, there is also a lot of material available elsewhere that you can use. We'll start by considering the resources available in your department. This chapter will help you to be more *organized* in your use of resources.

Psychology-specific Resources

Your psychology laboratories

In the United Kingdom, the British Psychological Society (BPS) requires that accredited degree courses have a psychology laboratory with appropriate technical support. Indeed, the BPS regularly visits accredited courses to ensure that the facilities are adequate for the number of students. But what can you find in a psychology laboratory that's useful to *you*? Well, many of the resources are primarily there to support research, but most are also used for teaching, especially for the final year project. Do find out if there is a laboratory handbook or set of relevant webpages available as these provide invaluable information about the laboratory resources available and how to use them.

The laboratories may include:

- **An observation room with a two-way mirror to enable observation of activities in a room (as in police dramas). These now tend to be used with video equipment that is either wall-mounted or fixed on a tripod.**

- **A psychophysics room that has appropriate light control so that it can be made to be completely dark.**

- **A room with facilities for recording biological measures such as galvanic skin response, heart rate and simple neural recording.**

- **Some psychology departments have access to animal facilities, but these are not usually used by undergraduate students except, perhaps, for undergraduate projects.**

In addition, you may well have access to computer facilities that give you access to a range of computer software, some of which you have probably used before. Common software packages that you are likely to use include:

- **A word processor, such as Microsoft Word, that you can use to produce essays and practical reports.**

- **A spreadsheet software, such as Microsoft Excel, that you can use for producing graphs or basic data analysis.**

- **A statistical package for analysing quantitative data that you collect in practicals. The most commonly used is SPSS (www.spss.com), which should be available for you to install on your home PC for free or for a nominal charge from your university's computer department.**

- **Analysis packages for qualitative data such as N6, the latest version of NUD*IST (www.qsrinternational.com).**

- **An Internet browser, such as Firefox or Internet Explorer.**

Psychology-specific software includes:

- **Data collection programs such as SuperLab (www.superlab.com), which the manufacturer describes as the 'best selling experimental lab software and experiment generator in psychology'.**

- **Various simulation programs. For example, there are a number of programs that enable you to test learning theories on a virtual rat.**

- **Similarly, there are also many programs that enable you to easily create a simple neural network.**

- **Various teaching programs. There are a lot of people studying psychology in the English-speaking world and there are a large number of programs specifically aimed at psychology students. Most of them are designed so that you can use them at your own pace, so it doesn't matter if you take more time than the other students or if you want to repeat exercises.**

It's worth asking the *laboratory staff* which programs are available as they are the ones who are in the best position to know.

Your student psychology society

Hopefully, your psychology department has a psychology society for undergraduate students. If it doesn't, you should try to set up one. However, note that student societies are something for students and so should be set up by students and not academic staff, although staff will normally provide any help they can.

What use is a psychology society? Well, it is an easy way to meet other psychology students, which can benefit your social life as well as your academic life. Often psychology societies organise guest speakers and visits that enable students to focus on the application of psychology to real-world problems, which can make a welcome change from the more academic orientation of your degree course. For example, your society may invite an admissions tutor for a post-graduate clinical psychology course to come to give a talk offering guidance on the nature of the course, on how to apply for a place and on the clinical psychology profession more generally. In addition, some psychology societies produce a magazine that tries to provide useful information, so watch out for that too. The psychology society may arrange a welcome event for new students, which conveniently enables current students to sell their old textbooks.

So, the psychology society can be a useful resource, but it can also be an impressive addition to your curriculum vitae if you help with its organisation. Helping run the society provides concrete evidence of your very real interest in psychology and of your organisational abilities.

Your national student psychology society

You should also check out the BPS Student Members Group (SMG) (www. smg.bps.org.uk). In essence, it provides the same opportunities as your own psychology society, but on a grander scale as you'll see from their website. As we explain in Chapter 9, the BPS SMG is a particularly good source of information about careers in psychology. You may also be interested in the European Federation of Psychology Students' Associations (EFPSA) (www.efpsa.org). EFPSA aims to promote the exchange of ideas and scientific cooperation among European psychology students, education throughout Europe in psychology, interaction among students and to facilitate mobility of European psychology students. Representatives of both the BPS SMG and EFPSA can get funding for attending international conferences, so there is another reason to get involved in them!

Professional bodies

In the United Kingdom, the professional body is, of course, the BPS. The BPS is keen to support undergraduate students in psychology and does so in a variety of ways. The annual student membership fee costs about the same as a non-chart CD. For that money, you get a copy of *The Psychologist* posted to you every month, with information about current issues in psychology as well as a copy of the BPS Appointments Memorandum, which contains details of job vacancies. The BPS also now produce a fortnightly email digest, to which anyone can subscribe, called 'Research Digest', that features recently published research that has been 'boiled down into tasty bite-sized chunks' together with relevant weblinks. It's also a great source of ideas for projects and may help you become interested in areas of psychology that you'd written off as dull, or that you haven't even heard about.

Libraries

If you were able to attend a university open day, it's almost certain that you were shown the university library and were able to gaze at floors of books. Historically, university libraries were just that – floors and floors of shelved books that scholars could read at nearby desks. However, this is now only a small part of the services that libraries provide. Many university libraries refer to themselves as part of the university's learning information services because they see themselves as enabling access to information of any sort. That information still includes books, but also includes journals, videos/DVDs and, very importantly, access to electronic resources.

Electronic resources (sometimes simply called 'e-resources') are increasingly important to anyone engaged in academic activity. It is essential that you are aware of the range of e-resources available to you as soon as possible, as that knowledge should make life a lot simpler for you. For example, rather than having to travel to a library, consult the catalogue to find if it holds a particular journal, go to the shelves to find it (and hope it hasn't been removed or mis-shelved), find a photocopier, work out how to use the photocopier and so on, you can often access papers from the comfort of your own computer and even print them out on your printer or save them to view at a later date.

The most obvious electronic database that you will need to use is your university's library catalogue. These are almost always available online so can be accessed from your home computer. We aren't going to try to explain how to use your library catalogue as they are all slightly different, but your library should have a fact sheet that helps you use their library catalogue. The important thing to note is that the library catalogue will provide listings not just of books, but also of journals and often other media such as newspapers, periodicals, videos/DVDs and even more unusual items such as sheet music.

There are a number of electronic databases that are used in psychology. Some are very expensive, but they are so useful that the majority of psychology departments pay for subscriptions. One produced by the American Psychological Association is PsycINFO (www.apa.org/psycinfo), which is a searchable database of abstracts, but not complete text, of psychological literature from the 1800s to the present.

Other useful resources include:

- **Social Science Information Gateway (www.sosig.ac.uk/Psychology)**

- **Web of Science (wos.mimas.ac.uk)**

- **Science Direct (www.sciencedirect.com).**

If you access to the last two via your university network, you may be able to download complete versions of papers. Whether you can depends on whether your university has a paper subscription to the journal or whether that journal is available online free to anyone at a UK university. Since most of these databases are expensive, it is usually the case that you need to be accessing them from the university's own network or using a password or some similar system. If you want to access the databases, specific journals or papers at home and have problems, contact your library to see if there is something extra that you need to do – don't just assume that you don't have that access.

How can the library staff help?

Some students see the library staff like supermarket staff: they stack the shelves and staff the checkout, scanning items for you. Certainly, those are two of their jobs, but library staff are actually highly skilled, with the typical librarian having a first degree and a relevant masters degree. Just like the academic staff, librarians enjoy helping students learn; in their case by helping students to access information. That can mean helping students to find relevant books, order inter-library loans or use subject-specific databases.

But what about all those books?

OK, the shelves and shelves of books are useful, particularly in some subjects such as fine art. For a psychology degree, however, you may find that the books are not as useful as articles. What usually happens with books is that the lecturer recommends one or two books that are very useful for completing an assessment. Unfortunately, there are often only a few copies of those books and over a hundred students wanting them. It's useful to remember that similar books are shelved together, so always have a look at other books in that section to see if there are other books that might be useful. One word of warning: old books tend to remain on bookshelves, even when they are past their use-by date, so avoid very old books.

Can I use another library?

You may live some distance from your university library and only travel in when you have timetabled activities. Fortunately, you can use other libraries. You can use your local library, but unless you are very lucky it won't have anything on academic psychology. However, it can still be a good place to work if you can find a quiet corner. What is more likely to be useful is another university library that is closer to where you live. You can find out about accessing these libraries using UK Libraries Plus (www.uklibrariesplus.ac.uk/students). As their website states: 'UK Libraries Plus is a co-operative venture between higher education libraries. It enables part-time, distance, and placement students to borrow material from other libraries. In addition, there is a provision for full-time students and for staff to use other libraries on a reference only basis. Membership is open to higher education institutions in the UK and nearly three-quarters are now members.' Also, if you are a member of the BPS you can, at no cost, access their psychology collection, which is the largest in Europe and is held in Senate House in London (www.ull.ac.uk).

My library doesn't have the book or paper that I want!

Students often become frustrated when they are unable to find the book or paper that they want in their library. However, there are an enormous number of new books and journals published every year and no library would be able to find space on the shelves for them, let alone pay for them. We've already described how you can use another library, if your university is a member of UK Libraries Plus (and most are). However, there is also a scheme called 'Inter-Library Loans', where books or a journal article can be obtained via the British Library (www.bl.uk). If you request a book, you will usually be sent a copy of the book, but if you request a paper, you would usually be sent a photocopy of that paper. Universities differ in their policy on undergraduates using inter-library loans, with some allowing only students doing a project to use the scheme. The cost is usually just a few pounds, but that is because the university subsidises the real cost which is more like £15. Your university library should have a fact sheet to help you.

Using the Internet (or Net)

We've already discussed use of specific e-resources, such as databases, but there is a huge variety of other information available on the net. Unfortunately, the net doesn't have an official catalogue like your library and, even worse, there are many unsavoury people after your mind or your money. However, there are a few useful tips that can make your use of the net more effective for your studies.

The first concern is *credibility* and is particularly important in psychology. Most bookshops, for example, have a section on psychology, but you will often find that it is actually a 'self-help' section. Some self-help books are excellent, but most are nonsense. Unfortunately, it's very difficult to know which is which (a good guide is checking that qualifications are genuine – someone called 'Dr' should either have a medical qualification or a PhD from a recognised university; if they don't, their advice isn't trustworthy). So, how can you know whether the information on a website is or isn't credible? You have one thing that can help you and that is the web address. You may have noticed that a number of the addresses we have given end in .ac.uk and such addresses indicate that the site is a recognised British academic institution; the equivalent in America is .edu. Therefore, the vast majority of material you will find on such websites is going to be acceptable. Be suspicious of information on *.com* websites as those are commercial websites and will try to sell you something. You should also be wary of *.org* (or *.org.uk*) sites as although some are learned societies (such as the BPS), others can be more questionable organisations.

The other concern is *relevance* and is obviously important; you want relevant material to help you understand an issue. To find relevant material, you need to use a *search engine*, but you need to be able to know how to search. The best search engine right now is Google (www.google.com), but feel free to try others. Let's consider an example of how to search.

Box 7:1   Searching the Net

Suppose you're interested in researching a topic in 'developmental psychology'. You might start searching by entering 'Developmental psychology'. If you use the quotation marks, Google will search for that exact phrase. Unfortunately, that gives you just under a million hits (searching for 'children' gives you a quarter of a *billion*!). It would not be good to try clicking on the links until you found what you wanted, so you have to be more specific.

Identifying the right search terms is one of the most useful skills to develop and it takes time to get the necessary experience, but here are a few tips.

1. *Use terms of the appropriate level of language*. Don't use 'booze' when you mean 'alcohol', that is, use the appropriate academic term.

2. *Don't be too specific*. Don't search for 'What are the causes of schizophrenia in Afro-Caribbean women'. Instead, search using 'schizophrenia', 'Afro-Caribbean' and 'women'.

3. *Try to add more search terms to restrict the number of outputs*. In the example above, if you just put in 'schizophrenia' you will get almost five million webpages, so you obviously need to be more precise. If you add 'Afro-Caribbean', then there are less than 5,000 hits found.

4. *Be prepared to try different words*. For example, you might be interested in schizophrenia in children, but might need to try searching using 'children', 'infants' and/or 'infancy'. You can use Google's advanced search to specify a list of words, any of which are appropriate.

5. *Remember American spellings*. For example, behavior instead of behaviour. Google is good at suggesting alternate spellings, which is useful in such cases and also if you misspell a word.

Finally, be careful when using material off the net in assessments that you don't accidentally plagiarise any material. See Chapter 6 for further information on plagiarism.

Buying Books

There is a great temptation when accepted on to a degree course to spend a lot of money (sometimes money you don't really have) on buying lots of books from a booklist. Don't do it! We've already mentioned in Chapter 1 that it's worth talking to students who have already completed the first year before buying books, unless you have been given strict instructions that you *must* buy particular books (and that's really rather rare).

Core Texts

Most units will specify a core text that must be bought. In psychology, you really should buy that book. You could try to be one of the lucky ones who gets hold of the core text from the library (check out last year's core text before the unit starts if you want to be among the first), but often you will find that another student requests it, so you can't keep the text for the duration of the unit. It's also tempting to try to share a book, and you might want to give that a go. We think that works only where you share a house so that it's easy to hand the book back and forth. The biggest problem is that you'll probably need the core text when you complete the coursework assignment, and most people do that at the same time – the last minute – so that can cause problems. Do remember that you should be able to sell most of your core texts to next year's students – if you don't go mad with a highlighter. That core text is important, as it should provide detail on particular topics so that you can prepare for teaching situations. It should also help you to construct the structure of a course-work essay and help with producing revision notes for examinations.

Most university campuses have a bookshop either on the campus or very close by. These university bookshops can be very good, providing a wide range of different books or little more than piles of core texts that are usually sold full price. If you are at a rural university, that bookshop might be the only one available to you. However, do remember that you will still have access to a wide variety of bookshops over the Internet. The most famous Internet bookshop, and used extensively by both of us, is Amazon (www.amazon.co.uk). Currently, if your order is for more than £15, Amazon delivers books for free and does accept cheques as well as debit and credit cards. Even better, Amazon and other Internet bookshops some-times have reductions on academic books, so you can save some money too. It's always worth checking with a price comparison site such as Kelkoo (www.kelkoo.co.uk) to see if another Internet bookshop is cheaper as prices can vary dramatically.

Beware of Old Books!

Psychology is still a relatively young discipline and old books can give a very mislead-ing impression of what most psychologists believe. For example, many books published in the 1960s take a very behaviourist view of psychology, but that is now an unpopular position. But what is an 'old' book? We would advise you to use books older than ten years with care. You can use them, but ensure that you also use material that is more up to date so that you can see if more recent research or theory has altered the relevance of that older material.

When buying a book, it is best to have the ISBN as well as the title, author(s) and publisher. You can find the ISBN on the page at the front that gives copyright and publishing information – look in this book for an example. It is also good to check whether there is more than one edition; this can very important for books that change between editions, for example, statistics books might refer to the current release of a statistics package.

Your Fellow Students

It is important that you don't think of your psychology degree as something that you do completely on your own. It's important when writing an essay or a practical report that you make sure that it is your own work, but at all other times do make use of other students' knowledge. When it comes to accessing resources, try to share your knowledge with other students. One of your colleagues may have discovered an excellent bookshop or a really useful website, so make sure that you regularly exchange such discoveries with each other. Also, do tell your lecturer, as they can then pass on that information to everyone.

Always Ask!

Finally, if you get stuck, do ask someone. For example, if a lecturer told you that you could use a particular set of computers at a particular time, but you are unable to do so, make sure that you let that lecturer know of the problem. If you email the lecturer, they can follow up that problem and hopefully solve it, but if they don't know about the problem, they can't do anything. Similarly, if there are resources that you think you and other students would find helpful, such as a computer program or a journal, do contact the most appropriate lecturer to see if it might be purchased. Always ask!

Box 7:2   Before You Move On ...

What resources are available in *your* psychology laboratory?

Do *you* have a psychology society?

What use is the BPS Student Members Group?

Have you got information sheets from *your* university library?

Where are the psychology books and psychology journals in *your* university library?

What databases can you access in *your* university?

What are the advantages and disadvantages of using the Internet?

8 The Psychology Project

Introduction

Why a whole chapter on 'The Psychology Project'? Well, your project is arguably the most important single piece of work that you will do in your psychology degree for a number of reasons. First, the project normally accounts for something like 20–25 per cent of your final degree classification and is often used to decide overall degree classification when a student is on a boundary between two grades, such as a lower second and upper second. Second, the project can be important in whatever you decided to do after your degree, as the admissions tutor for a masters degree might ask to read through it. Indeed, the tutor might be particularly interested in the mark you received for the project since it is the best piece of work for you to demonstrate your ability to organise yourself. Finally, your project supervisor is likely to be your main academic referee, so it is important to ensure that the student–supervisor relationship is as good as it can be.

A recently published book that was produced in conjunction with the British Psychological Society is also worth a look (and it only costs around £10):

Forshaw, M. (1994). *Your Undergraduate Psychology Project: A BPS Guide.* London: Blackwell.

But What is a Project?

A psychology project is a substantial piece of independent student-managed empirical work. The end result is a report of between 5,000 and 10,000 words produced in a very similar format to a journal article. It is a requirement of the British Psychological Society that a psychology project be empirical in nature. All 'empirical' means in this case is that it is centred on data that, in the vast majority of cases, you collect.

When our students hand in their projects, we ask them to give feedback on their experience of the project. One year we asked them to give one piece of advice to the students in the year below who would shortly be starting their own projects. In excess of 95 per cent, student gave advice along the lines of 'Start earlier than me!', 'Start early' and 'Make sure you are organised'. In short, the key to the success of your project is to *plan*. Yes, once again you need to think OCR.

O
C
R

Box 8:1   Using OCR in your Project

The project is the culmination of your studies, and is the major test of the extent to which you have mastered the skills of organisation, communication and reflection. *Organisation* is the first key to success. You are likely to work on your project for a year or more. While this might seem to give you plenty of time, it is easy to find that you are struggling to complete your project in time because you have frittered that time away due to bad project management. Your project report is almost certainly the longest single piece of work that you will produce on your degree. All of the points we have made about assessment being an act of *communication* apply 'in spades' with regard to the project. Finally, all stages of the project process will require concentrated *reflection* on what you are trying to achieve and on how your project is progressing.

Doing a project has the potential to be either the best experience of your degree or the worst! In this chapter we will give you advice so that you can increase the likelihood of the former occurring.

It's worth browsing this chapter at the start of your degree as the earlier you begin to think about your project the better. For example, if you wished to carry out research with children on the autistic spectrum, it would be extremely useful to have a part-time job working with such children in the year before starting the project. Similarly, if you want to work in a particular research area with a particular academic, then it is a good idea to attend relevant departmental seminars. For example, the lecturer may have invited a particular guest speaker to give a talk or may even give a talk themselves. If this happens you really should attend those talks so that you can find out more about that area. Another reason to go is so that the lecturer is likely to notice this and have positive feelings toward you, which is important if that lecturer is popular and can decide who will be, and who will not be, their project students.

Different departments will have different procedures for organising the final year project, but all will include a procedure for the allocation of students to supervisors. This is often the first step in the project process, since you will need to try to ensure that you are allocated a supervisor who has expertise and interests in the area in which you wish to work. Departments also differ on the extent to which you are given a relatively free choice of project topic and approach. Some departments, especially larger ones, will be able to support most topics and approaches. But some smaller ones may be more restrictive. Moreover, some departments have an 'apprentice model', where you work closely with a supervisor on an aspect of their current research. In this chapter we ignore these complications and assume that you have freedom to choose your own project topic and approach, but our guidelines should be useful regardless of the particular system your department uses.

Facing the Blank Page – Generating an Idea

By the time you get to your final year, you will have already experienced the problem of facing a blank page or, more likely, an empty 'new document' on your computer. If you have almost complete freedom, trying to choose an area can be very difficult. However, there are some strategies you can use that can make things easier.

Is there a part of the course that you particularly enjoyed?

As a starting point, you could think about a topic area that you particularly enjoyed, such as developmental psychology. However, within that topic area, try to narrow down your interest to material covered in a particular lecture, seminar or practical activity, or even an essay that you might have written. For example, you might have written an essay on Piaget's theory of cognitive development and have become very interested in conservation tasks: so, at what age do children pass the test of conservation of mass? An example of the conservation of mass test is when two identical balls of clay are presented and then one is rolled into a sausage shape and the child asked whether both clay shapes contain the same amount of clay. You may even have tried this out on your own or other people's children to see for yourself if you can replicate Piaget's findings. If you think you would be able to find children in the appropriate age range for a project, you might want to read further to see what the debates are in the *current* literature on this topic; Piaget's work is very much classic psychology so your project needs to focus on *current* debates, and to do that you must read the *current* literature. When you do that reading, make sure you are thinking critically and then you might come up with some starting points that you could discuss with a possible supervisor.

Another possibility is that you may be studying psychology in conjunction with another area (such as sociology, English or human resources) as part of a combined honours degree programme. It is possible that you may have a university degree in another area completely; for example, you might have a nursing degree and be very interested in the psychological mechanisms involved in stress. Indeed, that might be one of the reasons that you decided to do a psychology degree in the first place. If you are interested in the psychological aspects of a topic that you have studied in a non-psychological context, that could be another good starting point for a psychology project, but it is essential to remember that you will be completing a *psychology* project and *psychologists* will be assessing it! The greatest risk here is that you do a survey of a topic but never engage with the psychological literature and the theories associated with that topic.

What is happening in your life outside of your degree?

One of the advantages of studying psychology is that it does relate to real life, so it is possible to do a project that is inspired by what else is happening in your life. For example, some people decide to a psychology degree because of personal experience of a psychological issue. You may have experience with a child with learning difficulties, a person with dyslexia or someone with a mental disorder (such as depression, an eating disorder and so on). If you are still interested in that issue, then that could well be a good starting point. However, it is important to remember that your project should be an interest and not an obsession. Indeed, some psychologists are uncomfortable with students researching an area that is too close to them. An example would be a student who has suffered with depression and who is interested in doing a project on that topic. However, that would involve spending almost a year studying depression. There is a possibility that doing this could be a depressing experience and could lead to adverse outcomes.

Another possibility could be that you have noticed interesting differences between ethnic or religious groups. However, it is important to note that you need a theoretical psychological framework for these differences to be interesting to other psychologists. A good example would be if you wondered whether children raised as devout Muslims would perform better at a particular memory task compared to children brought up as strict Christians. The reason this question might arise for you is that Muslim children might develop better memory skills if they learn the Koran by heart.

The majority of full-time students probably have part-time jobs, and if you are studying part-time or on a distance learning course it is even more likely that you are in employment or doing unpaid voluntary work. Sometimes, these experiences can be used as a starting point for your project and even, as we'll see later, can provide you with participants.

Finally, other activities that you do when not studying can be a useful starting point. For example, you may be interested in flirting or risk-taking behaviour in pubs or clubs. You may have noticed that otherwise rational people engage in very risky behaviour in certain circumstances, such as having unprotected sex with someone they've just met in a pub or club.

In what areas of research are the academic staff active?

It is likely that many of your tutors are active in psychological research. If you don't already know what they are doing, you should be able to find out from your department's webpage or noticeboard. If neither of these provide that information, then you should ask for it!

What is in the news now?

Another possible source of ideas is current news stories. Over the course of your degree, you will have probably noticed that a large number of news stories have a psychological component. Indeed, you may well have seen reports claiming to document attitudes towards other people, for example, attitudes towards asylum seekers.

Other possibilities are the latest psychological news stories and recently published journal articles. Good examples of the former are reports of annual psychological conferences that are usually promoted by the national psychological association to promote psychology to the general population. Even more usefully, the British Psychological Society has recently started an email bulletin 'Research Digest' that provides a fortnightly round up of psychology research from across the globe. You can subscribe (for free) by emailing subscribe-rd@lists.bps.org.uk and you will then receive details of recent research. In each email there are normally about six studies listed, and here's an example of one such study:

> How do children feel about their transition from primary to secondary school? Ulrike Sirsch (University of Vienna, Austria) trialled a new questionnaire 'The Impending Transition to Secondary School Perceived as a Challenge and Threat (ITCT)' on 856 Austrian children, aged about 10yrs, before they were due to start secondary school.
>
> Grounding his research in Lazarus' theories of emotion, Sirsch found that 90 per cent of the children saw the transition as an academic challenge and nearly all of them saw it as a social challenge. A third of the children saw the transition as a social threat – they tended to be shy and to fear how others would react to them. Feeling academically threatened afflicted about half the sample and was more common among those children with low self-worth and a low sense of their own academic ability. High maths achievers were also more likely to feel academically threatened, presumably for fear of losing their current academic status. A prior visit to the new school protected against both forms of perceived threat.
>
> Sirsch concluded 'very few students in the present study perceived the transition from primary to secondary school as both a low challenge and a low threat. This confirms this transition as a significant and important life event for most of the children'.
>
> Sirsch, U. (2003). The impending transition from primary to secondary school: challenge or threat? *International Journal of Behavioural Development*, 27, 385–95.
>
> Journal weblink: www.tandf.co.uk/journals/pp/01650254.html
>
> Author weblink: www.iog.umich.edu/faculty/krause.htm

If you want to browse recently published journal articles, a good strategy is to identify the most appropriate journals in the library or available to you online. Then quickly read a few titles and perhaps the abstracts to get a feel for the sorts of things that seem most interesting to you.

How to focus in – an example

Suppose you are very interested in some research you have read on child sexual abuse and think that this would be an interesting topic for your project. The first issue you face is that it is highly unlikely you would be allowed to talk to actual victims of child sexual abuse. It would be ethically unsound for you to do so as you are unlikely to have gained the appropriate professional training to be able to do it in a sensitive way. So, you have to think creatively if you are to pursue this topic. You would, for example, be able to talk to members of the general public about their views on the victims and perpetrators of child sexual abuse and, for example, try to investigate what people think are the reasons why someone would commit such an act. Remember that you will need to relate that to existing psychological theories and not simply carry out a market research survey.

Ethics

It is essential to keep ethical concerns always in mind. The two main reasons why students cannot do their desired psychology project are that the idea is not ethical or it is not feasible. Your department will, for example, have a procedure for scrutinising the ethical soundness of your project, and it will refuse you permission to undertake the project if it is unethical in any shape or form.

So, as we illustrated above, it is important to note that different experiences or qualifications have an impact on what you can and cannot do. By the time you begin your project, you are unlikely to have the appropriate experience or expertise to work with potentially vulnerable groups (for example, those suffering mental distress) without direct supervision.

You can find ethical codes of conduct on the websites of most psychology associations:

- **American Psychological Association (www.apa.org)**

- **British Psychological Society (www.bps.org.uk) – click on 'The Society' and then 'Ethics'**

- **European Federation of Psychologists' Associations (www.efpa.be).**

Unfortunately, these ethical codes tend to be very long documents as they are provided to give comprehensive guidance and legal restrictions for the behaviour of psychologists. The most important principles are that your participants have given their informed consent, have the right to withdraw at any time and have the right to anonymity and confidentiality. Sometimes, you cannot reveal full details of your study before collecting data (although no deception is involved), so informed consent can be interpreted as whether the participant would be likely to agree to participate if they knew the full details of your study beforehand. An example of this is where you present slightly different vignettes (stories) to different participants where only one word might differ. The study would not work if you told everyone that you were manipulating, say, the gender of the main character. It is also important to debrief your participants at the end of your study, telling them anything that they want to know about your study. You should avoid deceiving your participants if at all possible, and you should seek the advice of your supervisor and/or your ethics committee if you want to use deception as part of the design of your study.

There are three basic ethical principles that operate for the project:

1. *Your participants must be protected*   It is essential that the physical and mental well-being of anyone who agrees to take part in your research be protected. It is very unlikely that you will be allowed to cause your participants any sort of distress, or administer any substances that could have negative outcomes. In particular, if your participants are children or members of a patient group, anything you do would be subject to great scrutiny.

2. *You must be protected*   It is essential that your project does not put you at risk. *Your* physical and mental well-being are important too. You would not be allowed to put yourself in a situation where you might be in danger. For example, you might mix socially with people who engage in illegal acts, but it is highly unlikely that you would be given permission to mix with them for your project.

3. *'Psychology'* must be protected   You will not be allowed to carry out tasks that require direct supervision (where that is not available). For example, you would not be allowed to interview psychiatric patients unless a suitable supervisory person was present.

Identifying Resource Needs and Support

Hardware

Hardware covers a wide range of equipment. If you are doing a reaction time study, you may well need a 'button box' to enable accurate recording of responses. These may be available, but are there *sufficient* available for everyone who wants one (or two)? Remember that other people (including other project students, research students doing PhDs and even members of academic staff) may want to use the same equipment and it would be very easy for a member of academic staff to use their influence to ensure that they, and not you, get the use of that piece of equipment. The best way of avoiding that problem is to obtain written confirmation (an email should be fine) that you can use a particular piece of equipment at the time you need it. Doing so may seem a bit of a fuss now, but it could save you a lot of hassle later.

Hardware requirements can include:

- Tape recorder for interviews (ideally one that allows pedal-controlled playback) with a high-quality microphone. If you are talking to more than one person, you may need more than one microphone and, ideally, a multi-channel tape recorder.

- **Video camera(s) for recording interviews or for an observational study. However, do check that the equipment you have is suitable for what you want to do. For example, will you be able to film unobtrusively in a suitable room?**

- **Button boxes or other response devices such as voice keys.**

- **Specific psychometric tests. You are not usually able to photocopy psychometric tests, so each copy needs to be purchased and their purchase can take time to organise.**

- **Access to a PC with appropriate software (see below) which is also suitable for data collection. You do not want participants doing a reaction time task if people are talking at the next PC.**

You may be fortunate to have specialised equipment in your psychology department, such as brain scanners, but you should discover at an early stage if these are available for student projects.

Software

There is a wide range of data collection packages for experimental research, and you should ensure that you know which packages are available for *your* use. Note that some of these packages are so expensive that your department may only have one copy, so you might need to book time to use that software. Do make sure that you have access to suitable supporting software, such as image manipulation software (for example, PaintShopPro or PhotoShop) if that is necessary. It is a good idea to glance through the manual for data collection packages and to talk to someone who has previously used any specific packages in which you are interested. If your department no longer has the manuals for a package, be very wary of designing your project around that package. Ideally, your department will have laboratory technicians who can help you with the basics of any packages they provide.

For qualitative research there are now a number of computer packages that assist in the analysis of transcripts. Again, you need to find out if suitable software is available for *your* use and if there is any help available for you.

Other resources

You might think that you do not need any resources for your project, but *where* are you intending to collect your data? You might think that 'any' room will do, but what you probably mean is a room that is:

- **Clean:** You don't want a room that smells of food, or worse, as that will probably be distracting and could result in some of your potential participants declining to continue to the end of the task.

- **Quiet:** It is even worth asking if any building work is planned for when you intend to collect your data.

- **Pleasant:** Not too hot and not too cold, and that can depend on when you intend on collecting your data.

- **Easy-to-find:** Your participants are usually giving up their time for free. If they find it difficult to find your room, they are likely to give up and not attend. If a room is difficult to find, make sure that you provide a map and clear directions, possibly even a contact number.

- **Bookable:** It would be a disaster if you had carefully set up a study only to find that other people were using that room at the same time. Ideally, you should book a room for which access is controlled (by a key or swipe card) and gain access a few hours earlier so that you can arrange furniture, lay out questionnaires or whatever you need to do.

- **Suitable for *your* needs:** You may need a very large room or a very small room, so it is important to think about what would be the best room, but also what would be acceptable. You would not want to do an interview in a very large, empty lecture theatre, as that could be unnerving for you and your interviewee.

You should think carefully about any other requirements that you might have. For example, if you will need to photocopy questionnaires, is there a facility available and is it funded for students projects?

Participants

Every year we have students who ask to use our 'research participation scheme' to recruit participants for their projects and specify that they require equal numbers of males and females. These students have failed to notice throughout their two previous years that more than 90 per cent of our psychology students are female! Having the right sort of participants is an important issue that is sometimes overlooked. It's no good having an excellent project idea which, for example, involves a single case study when that single case is not available. Similarly, if you do not already have access to a particular type of self-help group, it can be very difficult and very time consuming to gain that access. Therefore, you must consider the participants that realistically will be available to you and allow plenty of time to recruit them.

Developing Your Idea

The biggest problem in developing an idea is getting the balance right between trying to do too much and doing too little. If you attempt too much, you may be quickly overwhelmed and your project can end up incoherent and incomplete. On the other hand, if your project is not ambitious, it will probably be difficult to gain a high mark. Again, this is something that you need to discuss with a supervisor. You can use the box below to develop your idea.

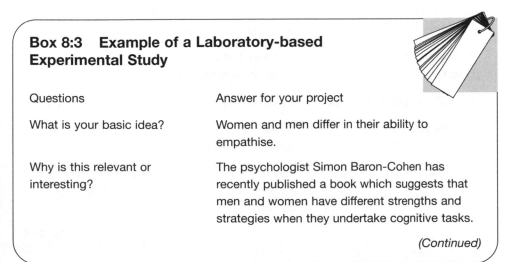

Box 8:2   Developing Your Idea

Questions   *Answer for your project*

What is your basic idea?
Why is this relevant or interesting?
What are your aims or predictions?
How will you collect your data?
Who will you study?
What resources do you need?
What will you measure?
Are these any ethical problems?

Over the next few pages we have completed some examples to demonstrate how to follow through an idea. However, do note that we have inserted only basic information and you might want to go into greater detail for your own project.

Box 8:3   Example of a Laboratory-based Experimental Study

Questions	Answer for your project
What is your basic idea?	Women and men differ in their ability to empathise.
Why is this relevant or interesting?	The psychologist Simon Baron-Cohen has recently published a book which suggests that men and women have different strengths and strategies when they undertake cognitive tasks.

(Continued)

Box 8:3 (Continued)

What are your aims or predictions?	Women will be better at empathising compared to men. Therefore, women's reaction times for an emotional Stroop task will be slower compared to men.
How will you collect your data?	Participants read a story that involves highly emotional goings-on. Then, they do an emotional Stroop task using words that correspond to the emotions generated in the story.
Who will you study?	Undergraduates.
What resources do you need?	PC, software for running a Stroop task (perhaps a button box or voice key).
What will you measure?	Reaction times to the Stroop task.
Are there any ethical problems?	Nothing special.

Box 8:4 Example of a School-based Observational Study

Questions	*Answer for your project*
What is your basic idea?	The nature of play is related to academic achievement.
Why is this relevant or interesting?	The ways in which children play may be related to their cognitive development.
What are your aims or predictions?	Children who are the highest achievers will show more imaginative play.
How will you collect your data?	By observing children during their play periods.
Who will you study?	Children in a particular year at a school to which I believe I have access.
What resources do you need?	Access to children and possibly video-recording equipment to enable more effective coding of behaviour.

(Continued)

Box 8:4   (Continued)

What will you measure?

The nature of children's play: whether they play alone or together, the range of their activities etc. Coding will be based upon a pilot study where the types of play will be observed and categorised. In addition, either a simple test of intelligence will be used or student records used if they are available.

Are there any ethical problems?

Will need written permission from the Head Teacher and must keep observations anonymous and confidential.

Box 8:5   Example of a Qualitative Study

Questions

Answer for your project

What is your basic idea?

Partners' perceived quality of sexual encounters influences the perceived overall quality of a romantic relationship.

Why is this relevant or interesting?

The topic of sexual satisfaction, although important, has been marginalised in academia yet is extensively covered in the media.

What are your aims or predictions?

No specific predictions, but aim to document participant-defined understandings about sexual satisfaction and quality of romantic relationship.

How will you collect your data?

Using semi-structured interviews or focus groups.

Who will you study?

Couples in long-term (greater than six months) romantic relationships.

What resources do you need?

Tape recorder, transcriber and suitable interview room.

(Continued)

Box 8:5   (Continued)

What will you measure?   No particular measurements, but interviews will be
                                         transcribed and themes identified and discussed.

Are there any ethical problems?   Will need to ensure that interviewees are assured
                                         of confidentiality and anonymity. In particular, it
                                         must not be possible to identify participants from
                                         information (i.e. extracts) used to illustrate themes.

Managing Your Supervisor

An important reason for focusing on your relationship with your project supervisor is that your supervisor is often one of the people whom you will ask to write your academic reference on graduation. So the quality of the relationship that you build up with him or her can have an effect on your future prospects. For example, if you are always late and disorganised for meetings, always fail to meet deadlines that you and your supervisor have agreed, and generally show little commitment to your project, then how good do you think your reference is likely to be?

Meetings with your supervisor

The advice we gave in Chapter 3 on managing relationships with tutors applies in this context too. We suggested earlier in the book that you would be well advised to construct an agenda for any tutorial meeting, but for a meeting on your project it is *essential*. Creating an agenda might sound complicated, but it isn't. It's like seeing your GP, where you would want to have said certain things and, crucially, would not want to leave until you'd had answers to your questions and had resolved some issues. You should write down your agenda, normally consisting of specific questions and should consider letting your supervisor have the agenda or those questions in advance so that they have the opportunity to think over the issues.

In the meeting itself, you should be prepared to provide a clear but brief overview of where you are in your project. Recognise that your supervisor will usually not just be supervising you. He or she may have a number of undergraduate and graduate students to supervise and so may need to be reminded of exactly what you are doing and of the stage you have reached. Your agenda should contain questions that are as specific as possible. It is much better to ask, 'I don't understand Baddeley's rationale for undertaking experiment E [give details] on the phonological loop in working memory', rather than 'I don't understand experiment E' or, even worse, 'I don't understand all that phonological loop stuff'.

And, of course, remember what we said in Chapter 3 about the necessity to take notes in the meeting and of putting some time aside for reflection after the meeting.

Email contact

Some, but not all, supervisors use email as part of their supervision. If your supervisor does use email then it can be an excellent way to check details of what you intend to do for your project. However, don't send dozens of emails, and avoid asking questions that would require lengthy emailed answers!

Managing Your Time

The biggest risk with the project is allowing it to run out of control. It is absolutely essential that you plan the entire project and regularly monitor your progress. Again, you need OCR. Organisation is the key to success in the project, and the most important thing to realise is that the project process is not a serial one. Doing a project does mean working through the five stages that we have listed in serial order below:

1. **obtain literature**

2. **identify hypotheses or research questions**

3. **collect data**

4. **perform analyses**

5. **write up.**

But that's not what a project is really like. Instead, take a look at Figure 1 below, which outlines a typical workplan for a laboratory-based experimental project. Note that we've identified six keys areas in which activities take place in parallel. Let's consider each of those six areas in turn for this particular workplan.

Literature review

It is very easy to think of the literature review as being something that you do once. Nothing could be further from the truth. You should identify and read key papers to

Area	Specific activities			Time →		
Literature review	Identify and read key papers and put in order for others	Read more papers		Ensure all relevant literature has been obtained and included in your literature review		
Managing participants	Check arrangements for recruitment	Recruit for pilot study		Recruit for main study		
Data collection	Book laboratory facilities	Produce stimuli	Pilot study		Main study, ensuring that data is properly recorded	
Analysis			Plan analysis (explicitly!)			Perform main analysis
Writing up	Produce draft of aims and method (and introduction)	Complete method and aims		Produce results and discussion sections		Pull together complete project
Supervisor	Discuss ideas and plan study	Review pilot study		Review main study		Review draft

Figure 1 A typical workplan for a laboratory-based experimental project

enable you to put together your basic idea for the project, but you should then follow up some of the literature cited in those key papers that are relevant to what you are investigating. You may find, for instance, that when you are planning your data collection you need to obtain other literature to help you in stimuli production or how to measure a particular effect. Also, note that papers are published all the time so you need to check every month or so whether articles relevant to your project have been published. Finally, note that you might have to order a paper using an Inter-Library Loan and that can take time.

Managing participants

It is important to timetable how you will recruit participants as well as how you will timetable data collection with them. For example, you might need to check that you have sufficient credit to use a research participation scheme. You also need to time your requests for participants with care because if you ask for volunteers too early before you are collecting data, your participants are unlikely to remember that they have agreed to take part, but if you ask people too late, they may not be available when you need them. You will need to make a judgement on the timing dependent on the people who will be participating.

Data collection

It is very important not to be too optimistic about the data collection process. Even something as 'simple' as producing your stimuli might take a great deal of time, for example, if you are forced to produce individual files for 400 presentations. The pilot study is likely to highlight problems with data collection packages, but solving those problems may not be trivial.

It is also important to realise that although your experiment may take only 30 minutes to complete, you may need to allow more time than that for each participant. If you plan to collect data from 9.00 a.m. to 5.00 p.m. each day for a week and as a result think you will be able to collect data from 80 participants, you are going to be disappointed. You *will* have problems – with rooms, equipment, your transport, people turning up late, people not turning up at all, people misunderstanding instructions and people not taking the experiment seriously. You need to ensure that you leave some time between people, not least so you can give them a debriefing, answer their questions and perhaps complete any research participation scheme forms. Do make sure you allow yourself time for toilet breaks, tea/coffee breaks and that you will be able to eat something during the day – it is very easy to forget to explain some important aspect of the experiment if you haven't eaten. You should allow some extra time in case preparing stimuli, programming the study or learning how to use the equipment takes longer than you expected or you catch a bad cold or have a domestic crisis.

Analysis

That'll take an afternoon, won't it? Oh no, that's very unlikely! Before collecting *any* data, you should have planned your main analysis. By main analysis, we mean the analysis that you need to answer your main research questions. You must ensure that the data you are collecting are suitable for the analysis that you have planned. For an experimental project, this is the most important thing to check. If you get this wrong, you are sunk! In addition to the main analysis, you should expect to have to explore the data, particularly if you don't get the results that you expected. In that case, you should try to work out what else could have happened and be prepared to seek evidence for that explanation in your data. That is a good reason why you should collect as many types of measures as you can, for example, reaction times as well as whether a response is correct so that you could look at those other measures if necessary. If you haven't collected that response, you would not be able to examine it without running the experiment again.

You might find that you have tried a variety of different approaches to your data and that you want to do the definitive analysis straight through on a raw set of data to ensure that you have not made any mistakes. It should go without saying, but data exploration is most definitely *not* about trying every statistical test on your data and looking for any that give significant results. That is a recipe for disaster!

Writing up

If you try to write up in the final week, you will find the experience very painful and very frustrating. It is important to produce drafts of each of the sections as soon as you can. In part, producing drafts is a good idea because if you cannot write a fairly detailed Method section before you collect your data, it suggests that you haven't really worked out what you are going to do. For example, you may not have thought about the inter-stimulus interval that you are going to use, but if you are specifying in explicit detail the experimental procedure you may realise that omission. If you have to produce a project proposal you may find that a useful starting point for the project report itself.

Supervisor

You should consult your supervisor as and when necessary, but it is worthwhile to plan particular times when you would want to see them. For example, it is a very good idea to discuss what you have learnt from your pilot study and to review your main study as soon as possible. In addition, it is good to find out if your supervisor is prepared to read a draft of your project (normally excluding the Discussion section) and give you feedback on that.

How would the workplan differ if I were undertaking a non-experimental project?

Each project will have a slightly different workplan. However, for non-experimental projects we can identify some general differences from the plan we have provided above. The main differences will be found in the Managing participants, Data collection and Analysis sections.

For an *observational study*, at a school for example, you will probably need to ensure that you have arranged to gain access as soon as possible. You need to take great care to ensure that you know exactly what you are doing for the main study as you may have only one opportunity to collect data. For that reason it is a good idea to have a number of small-scale pilot studies. For example, you might want to practise coding behaviour on adults first and then your own or a friend's children.

For a *questionnaire study* you may find that data collection is relatively quick and easy, but coding the data might take a great deal of time. The subsequent analysis might be more complicated and involve segmenting your sample in a variety of different ways, so you might have to allow more time for the analysis. If you are designing your own questionnaire, you will probably need to allow quite a bit of time for the pilot study (or studies) to ensure that your questionnaire is both valid and reliable.

For a *qualitative study* you should expect to spend far more time on coding the data and performing the analysis compared to data collection itself. But even before you can do this you will have to transcribe the interviews that you have recorded. This is a major drain on your time. The major difference in terms of planning for qualitative rather than quantitative studies is that for the former the time-consuming work occurs primarily *after* the data are collected. In contrast, in quantitative studies the time-consuming work occurs primarily in preparing for data collection and collecting the data.

Note that the workplan we have provided ignores a number of important things that you will need to include in your workplan:

- *Ethics procedures* Timetabling issues are particularly important if you have to get involved with an external ethics procedure (for example, a school or hospital). Often, the ethics committee will meet only at particular times of the year, take longer to give permission and may have different requirements from your department's procedures.

- *Proposal submission* As part of the project process you may have to submit a project proposal, so you will need to timetable for that too.

- *Other academic work* You will probably be attending lectures, seminars and tutorials for a number of other parts of the degree. You may also have other assessments, such as essays, practical reports and examinations, that are also important and require your time. Your plan needs to take them into account too.

- *University timetable* The university is likely to be closed at Christmas and Easter. You may not observe those holidays, but in the United Kingdom you will normally find that universities close down over those periods and the academic staff disappear to attend conferences, work on their research and even to see their families.

- *The rest of your life!* You may well have one or more part-time jobs to fund yourself during your degree. It is worth noting that some students try to give up their part-time jobs for the final few months of their degree so that they can really focus. If that is feasible for you, you may want to consider it. However, don't forget your personal life and the lives of those close to you. You need to allow time for partners, parents, children and friends for your benefit as well as theirs. Don't let those relationships suffer when you're doing the project, as you will find it easier to do the project if you allow yourself some time for relaxation.

Plagiarism

We have already mentioned this, but it is worthwhile mentioning it again in this chapter because of the possible consequences. The project usually counts for something like 20 per cent of the final degree mark and if failed (as can happen if plagiarism is detected) then your degree may be awarded without honours. In the worst cases, a plagiarised project can result in expulsion and no degree at all being awarded.

Given the above, it is clearly incredibly foolish to plagiarise deliberately. So, the biggest risk is probably that you plagiarise unintentionally, but remember that this too can be severely punished. Unintentional plagiarism is a particular risk in the project because the work is spread over such a long period – up to a year in some cases – that it is easy to forget the original source for your notes. To avoid that danger, you should always note the original reference whenever you copy directly from a source, whether that copy was made onto paper or into a computer document.

The Final Project Report

To some extent, the project itself is a beefed-up practical report that is almost a scientific paper. Some psychology departments actually require the project to be in the form of a scientific paper. Therefore, the best advice for producing the final report is to look at published work in the field in which you are doing your project. That normally means looking at the style used in the journals that you have included in your references.

There are different emphases for each section when writing up the project, but the structure of the project is normally very similar to the practical reports that you will have previously completed. So you should look back at the section on writing up practical reports in Chapter 6 when you come to start writing up. In addition, you *must* make sure you meet any specific requirements made by your department that go beyond the general requirements we have discussed.

Are there any major differences if I am writing up a qualitative study?

There is a very useful paper on 'Evolving guidelines for publication of qualitative research studies in psychology and related fields' (Elliott, Fisher and Rennie, 1999). It is a paper that you should read if you are doing a project that involves the presentation of qualitative data, but also one you should read if you are interested in having a broader perspective on psychology. You should try to find and access this paper using your university's online facilities. Below you have all the information that you need to track down that paper. If you cannot, then you should seek the advice of a member of library staff on searching databases as a matter of urgency!

Here's the complete reference for this journal article:

Elliott, R., Fisher, C.T. and Rennie, D.L. (1999). Evolving guidelines for publication of qualitative research studies in psychology and related fields. *British Journal of Clinical Psychology 38*, 215–29.

Elliott and colleagues highlight seven 'publishability' guidelines that are shared by both qualitative and quantitative approaches. These are:

1. **explicit scientific context and purpose**

2. **appropriate methods**

3. **respect for participants**

4. **specification of methods**

5. **appropriate discussion**

6. **clarity of presentation**

7. **contribution to knowledge**

In addition, they give seven 'publishability' guidelines that are particularly relevant to qualitative research. These are:

1. **owning one's own perspective**

2. **situating the sample**

3. **grounding in examples**

4. **providing credibility checks**

5. **coherence**

6. **accomplishing general vs. specific research tasks**

7. **resonating with readers.**

Elliott and colleagues explain in detail what they mean by each of these guidelines in their paper, but you should have a good idea of the issues with which they are concerned from the list above.

General appearance

The project should impress with its content and not by the packaging, although clear and neat presentation is important. Avoid the temptation to use leather covers, fancy paper and especially avoid the temptation to use elaborate fonts! You should use standard quality, clean white A4 paper and a standard font (usually Times New Roman) at the standard font size (usually 12 point) and usually double-line spaced. The only elaboration that you should allow yourself is sparing use of **bold**, *italics* and <u>underlining</u>. Try to avoid the use of exclamation marks as these are rarely effective, as they tend to make the writer look immature when used in a formal research document.

Title

This is the very first thing of note that the markers will read, so try your best to ensure that it has a positive, and not negative, impact. Once again, you should look at published articles in peer-reviewed journals. It is safest to avoid a 'clever' title that is intended to be funny, as that can easily irritate the marker.

Abstract

As usual, the title is followed by the Abstract, but this time the Abstract is especially important. Anyone who is reading your project is going to begin forming their opinions based on the first thing they read which, after the title, is the Abstract. If the Abstract is weak, and the Abstract can be difficult to write, then that is not a good start and you probably already know about the primacy effect …

Introduction

The Introduction to a project is different to the sort of introduction that you have probably written for previous practical assessments. For the project, you need to briefly introduce the general area before focusing on the particular area that you are investigating. In particular, you need to bring out the theoretical issues that belong specifically to the *psychological* study of your topic and so highlight debates in the psychological literature that relate to the particular question that you are attempting to address. You need to conclude by clearly identifying your hypotheses or research questions, and these should follow logically from the literature you have reviewed. Remember that the markers will be most interested in what it is *exactly* that you are trying to do, so it is very important that you make the final paragraph crystal clear.

Method

The major difference in the Method section compared to those that you have written before is the level of detail required and the complexity of what you did. For example, if you carried out a pilot study you would need to indicate what you did and how that altered the way you carried out the main study. The other major difference is that the project could be the first time that you have carried out a study where the marker really doesn't know what you did. If you think back to experiments that you did in level 1, the marker probably knew almost exactly what you did and/or may even have a marking schema that identifies key points that need to be mentioned. However, for the project the marker is looking for you to tell them exactly what you did so that they can understand how you collected your data.

Results

Again, the major difference in the Results section is likely to be the complexity of what you have done compared to reports that you have previously completed. For example, it *might* be appropriate to present some information about your participants, for example, a bar chart or table of their occupations. Rather than one statistical test, you may use a variety of descriptive and inferential statistics. Rather than one figure or table, you may use a combination of figures and tables. The important thing is to ensure that you have completely explored the data that you collected, but the presentation should be exhaustive and not exhausting. For example, it is not appropriate to present a bar chart showing the number of male and female participants in your study. It is also not appropriate to give pages of near-identical graphs when you fail to find statistical significance using the appropriate statistical tests.

Potentially, your Results section could be quite a few pages in length, so don't be afraid to use subheadings to help organise yourself and to assist the marker. It is helpful to think of the Results section as an opportunity to lead the reader through your analyses.

Things to remember for the presentation of qualitative data

While presentation of quantitative data is essentially quite straightforward and follows standard procedures, the situation for the presentation of qualitative data is more fluid. Do make sure that you read Elliott *et al*. (1999) and talk to your supervisor about the best way to present *your* results.

Discussion

The Discussion is particularly important for the project. This is where you have the opportunity to bring everything together and really demonstrate your abilities in critical thinking. It's normally the last thing that the marker reads (though we know some markers who always read the Discussion first). If it is the last thing the marker reads before deciding on their mark for your project, it is essential that you make a good impression (and you should know by now about the recency effect). Therefore, you must deal with any inconsistencies as explicitly as you can. Within reason, you should be prepared to admit that you couldn't find a convincing explanation for any really puzzling results. However, you should see this as an opportunity to display your abilities to really understand empirical data and be able to relate data to theory.

References

Ensure that the References are produced according to your department's guidelines. Make sure that any work you cite in the text has a corresponding reference in this section, but also that you make sure that there are no references that are not referred to in the text. One word of caution: avoid the temptation to bulk out the reference section. When there are a large number of references, the marker is less likely to believe that you have read all the references and therefore may look more carefully in the text for evidence that you have read and *understood* your references.

Appendices

With the project, Appendices tend to be too large rather than too small. Resist the temptation to include too much material. Some departments do require the inclusion of statistical output, but otherwise do not include this material. Items that should be included in Appendices are:

- **A questionnaire that *you* produced and used, but not a standard questionnaire.**

- **An interview plan that you used to help you with every interview.**

- **Word-lists.**

- **Visual stimuli (indicative *samples* if too numerous).**

Other materials

Make sure that you are clear as to whether any other information or materials are required in your submission. These items could include a copy of:

- **The project on computer disk or CD.**

- **The data or statistical spreadsheet and/or analysis for quantitative work.**

- **The transcripts of interviews for qualitative work.**

- **Any video material that was presented to participants on VHS or DVD.**

- **Data collection computer programs.**

- **Official letters giving permission to collect data at schools, hospitals and so on.**

Understanding How the Project is Assessed

You should feel a real sense of achievement when you hand in your project, as it will be the culmination of almost a year's work. But you shouldn't forget that it is not an end in itself. As we said at the beginning of this chapter, the mark you are awarded for your project carries a great deal of weight in the determination of your final degree classification, so it is worth understanding how projects are assessed.

In the main, the same guidance can be given on the assessment of the project as on the assessment of any work – so you should read the section on practical reports (pp. 76–89) in Chapter 6 again where we discussed this. But there are one or two differences that might be of interest.

Normally, the project is double-marked, which means that two separate markers (one of whom may be your supervisor) read through it and give it a mark, and this is not always the case with other assessments. The two markers will then compare their individual marks. You may be surprised to hear that, more often than not, they agree exactly, that is, 'this is a solid, high 2:2'. Students are sometimes surprised that markers, sometimes with very different backgrounds within psychology, can agree so often. But there can be disagreements, and if there is your project may be marked by a third marker and examined by one of the external examiners.

Markers will generally not be too worried if your study has not produced a statistically significant result, unless they think this is due to incompetence or carelessness on your part. They are interested in seeing how well you have demonstrated the capability to design, undertake and report on a larger piece of empirical work. They may well also consider a report from your supervisor on how much input they had to make to get you through the project process. Obviously, if your supervisor reports that you needed a great deal of help, then you will tend to get a lower mark, since the project is meant to be an independent piece of work.

Taking the Project Further

Some departments require production of a poster based on the project; some departments require delivery of a talk on the project: some even demand both a talk and a poster. In addition, some projects are of such good quality that you may be advised to produce a poster or a talk for a scientific conference or a paper for publication. You may even want to use your project as the basis for further research leading to the award of a research masters degree or PhD. Below, we give some general advice on how to carry out these tasks.

Producing a poster for a presentation (internal and external)

In Chapter 6 we provided some guidelines for producing a poster. These also apply for the project, but remember that you are likely to be the expert on your topic. The danger here is that you assume too much knowledge on the part of the reader as you have spent so long focussed on the project itself. It is a very good idea to have a friend (maybe another project student) look at your poster panels to see if they can follow what you have done. The other danger is that you attempt to fit the entire project onto a poster. Do remember that you are usually available during a poster presentation time-slot to answer questions, and you should always provide contact details in case anyone wants to ask any follow-up questions.

Producing a talk for a presentation (internal and external)

In the previous chapter we also provided some guidelines for giving an oral presentation. The major difference for an oral presentation for your project is that you are likely to be the expert on that topic, maybe even more so than your supervisor. After all, you should have read a number of relevant papers in some detail and have been working on your topic for almost a year. Fortunately, that means that the experience should actually be less stressful compared to giving a talk in a seminar. Otherwise, the advice on giving an oral presentation remains unchanged. The most important thing is to keep things simple and try to tell a story. Make it clear:

- **What your project was about.**

- **Why you did it.**

- **What your aims/hypotheses were.**

- **What you did.**

- **What you found.**

- **What you conclude.**

It's often worthwhile to highlight the problems that you encountered (and hopefully overcame), but resist the temptation to use an oral presentation to settle scores or to try to name someone publicly who did not help you as much as you expected. Do remember to find the presentation method that works best for you, and ensure that any overheads are clear and easy to read. You can always give handouts with diagrams that would be difficult to see when using PowerPoint or overhead transparencies.

Producing a paper for publication

If your project is of a sufficiently high standard and the results would be interesting for a wider audience, you may want to consider submitting a paper for publication. You should discuss the feasibility of doing so with your supervisor as it can involve a fair amount of work and take a considerable length of time to complete the peer-review process. It is also advisable to agree as soon as possible the order of the authors of the paper. If the supervisor provided you with the project idea, gave a lot of help and then wrote the paper, they would probably expect to be first author. However, if you came up with the project idea and make a substantial contribution to the paper, then it is reasonable for you to be first author. There are APA guidelines, but it's easier to avoid upset by discussing authorship as early as possible!

Developing the project into a research masters or PhD

You may have enjoyed your project so much that you want to take it further, by doing more research on that topic. In fact, that's how most academics end up becoming academics (you didn't think it was for the money, did you?). For example, you might be interested in doing a PhD with your supervisor with the project as a starting point. However, you might want a change of scene and prefer to move somewhere else, but continue with research in that field. In that case, talk to your supervisor as soon as possible. They may not want to make the commitment (at least three years) of supervising research at your university on that particular topic. Let's be honest, they may not want to supervise you!

Alternatively, you may have enjoyed the process of doing research, but don't wish to take your project idea further. Instead, you may want to do research on a slightly different topic or in a completely different area. In that case, you should be aware of emails or notices advertising research studentships at suitable institutions both in the United Kingdom and abroad. Don't be reticent in emailing academics with whom you would like to do a PhD. It's flattering to receive such enquiries and the worst that could happen is that you don't get a reply. Once again, do talk to an academic in your department who works in that field as they may have suggestions for ways to take your interests forward.

Be aware, though, that it is likely that you will need at least a good upper second to receive funding to undertake a PhD.

Box 8:6 Before You Move On ...

What are some of the strategies for coming up with a project idea?

What resources (hardware, software, expertise and people) are available to you?

How might ethics affect what you can do?

What activities need to be included in your workplan?

Do you have a detailed workplan?

What are the specific requirements of *your* department for your project?

9 Future Directions

LEARNING OUTCOMES

1. To be aware of your post degree options, including careers inside and outside of psychology.
2. To be aware of the training required, job descriptions and sources of further information for careers that have chartered status within the British Psychological Society.

Introduction

We hope you are *not* reading this chapter while clutching your newly awarded degree certificate. Ideally, as we advised at the start of the book, you should read this chapter as early as possible in your degree. In fact, it would be good to read this chapter *before* starting a degree in psychology. The reason for reading this is that it will help you to make the right choices on your degree course so that you are best prepared for the particular career path on which you have set your heart. For instance, suppose you want to do a masters in health psychology. It would probably be useful to take an optional course in health psychology if there is one available in your final year, to consider doing your project on a health-related topic, and talking to any chartered health psychologists in your department about what this particular career path involves.

O
C
R

Box 9:1   Using OCR in Career Planning

As we have stressed throughout this book, it is important to *organise* for your future career as soon as you are ready, to *communicate* with others who know more in order to seek their help and advice, and to *reflect* on what you discover to ensure you are following a path that is genuinely the right one for you.

Seeking Advice

One of the biggest problems in choosing what you would like to do with your degree is being unaware of the possibilities that are available to you. Some of your lecturers may be chartered psychologists and so have experience of one of the professional areas. However, strange as it may sound, many of your lecturers may not know much about professional careers in psychology. We are sometimes asked what it is like to work as, say, an occupational psychologist. However, neither of us has worked as an occupational psychologist, nor have we received any training in that area. In other words many lecturers, like us, will be familiar with what is involved in being an academic psychologist, but might have no direct experience of any other field. Remember also that we have chosen to be academic psychologists above any of the other possibilities, so our views are naturally biased. So who or what will give you the information you need? Fortunately, you have a number of other reliable sources for advice.

A very good starting point is to obtain the latest careers booklet from the British Psychological Society (www.bps.org.uk). Their careers booklet currently gives information on careers in: clinical psychology, counselling psychology, educational psychology, forensic psychology, health psychology, neuropsychology, occupational psychology and teaching and research in psychology.

But the BPS careers booklet can only be your starting point as many of the various options may be equally interesting to you. A good next move is to attend talks from experts in their field that will be given as part of your psychology department's seminar series. If your department does not have relevant speakers, find out the programme for neighbouring psychology departments and also see if there are relevant talks at neighbouring hospitals. You can also look out for BPS events (www.bps.org.uk) where guest speakers talk about their research interests. The BPS website is a great source of information, but do make sure that you look at the webpages from the BPS Student Members Group (www.bps.org.uk/smg) as they provide a number of interviews with admissions tutors and psychologists working in particular areas. Another good idea is to see if there are any positions (paid and unpaid) working with psychologists so that you have an opportunity to see their daily working lives. Finally, newspapers like the *Guardian* (www. guardian.co.uk) have regular features on different careers and these include psychology.

Careers Not Directly Related to Psychology

You are also in an extremely good position if you decide to work outside of psychology. Psychology is arguably one of the best for developing the general skills that are most sought after by employers in a wide range of graduate entry-level jobs. That claim is not psychologists demonstrating unwarranted arrogance, but rather a reflection of the topics covered and the methods used in a psychology degree. Consider some of the skills developed in a psychology degree:

- **essay writing**

- **report writing**

- **data entry and manipulation**

- **statistics**

- **computer use (Internet, word processing and statistics)**

- **critical thinking.**

Possible careers include market research, social work, teaching, nursing, advertising, sales, media and broadcasting, personnel management and even the police and the armed forces. However, any job that specifies a requirement for any university degree would almost certainly be suitable for someone with a psychology degree.

Here are some suitable starting points for exploring careers not requiring a psychology degree:

- **Official Graduate Careers website (www.prospects.ac.uk)**

- **Graduate jobs and career advice (www.doctorjob.com)**

- **Public and voluntary sector jobs and careers (www.getalife.org.uk)**

- **The National Council for Work Experience (www.work-experience.org)**

- **Careers in Local Government (www.lgcareers.com)**

- **Civil Service Recruitment Gateway (www.careers.civil-service.gov.uk)**

- **NHS Careers (www.nhscareers.nhs.uk)**

- **Teacher Training Agency (www.tta.gov.uk); UK teaching jobs and careers in teaching (www.tesjobs.co.uk)**

- **The police and criminal justice job site (www.bluelinecareers.co.uk)**

- **Social work recruitment campaign site (www.socialworkcareers.co.uk)**

- Forces: Army (www.army.mod.uk); Navy (www.royalnavy.mod.uk); Royal Air Force (www.raf.mod.uk)

- The Market Research Society (www.mrs.org.uk/careers/career.htm)

- Institute of Practitioners in Advertising (www.ipa.co.uk)

- Sales and Marketing (www.sales-and-marketing-jobs.co.uk).

Careers Directly Related to Psychology

The best news for you is that the future for careers in psychology looks very rosy. In most Western countries, psychology is becoming increasingly important in health care and related fields and some careers, such as sports psychologist, did not even really exist a few years ago. It is likely that completely new careers in psychology are going to develop in the near future and there is every reason to think they will continue to be relatively well paid.

Important things to do for success:

- Locate information about possible careers as early as possible.

- Find out about relevant conferences and talks.

- Read at least one serious book on a particular area of psychology.

- Make sure you have relevant voluntary or paid experience.

- Get the most out of your undergraduate degree (that is, optional units chosen, project area).

- Join the relevant division of the BPS.

- Find out as much as you can about the selection procedures for relevant courses.

- Demonstrate enthusiasm in your interview.

Careers Currently Chartered by the BPS

Clinical psychology

What does a clinical psychologist actually *do*? Clinical psychologists typically work as part of the NHS, but some are in private practice. Their work involves reducing psychological distress and improving psychological well-being. Problems dealt with include: anxiety, depression, eating disorders, compulsive behaviours, dealing with a physical illness, childhood behaviour disorders, relationship problems (including those within families) and other mental health issues. Clinical psychologists usually work as part of a team (with other health professionals or social workers) and normally make a clinical assessment using observation and perhaps psychometric tests before devising and implementing a course of therapy, counselling or other advice.

Clinical psychology is one of the most popular post-graduate options and competition for places is very fierce. Universities offering clinical courses want applicants to have a good psychology degree accredited by the BPS as providing Graduate Basis for Registration (GBR). By a good degree, we mean that you have a first class or upper-second degree. If you achieve a lower-second degree, you would usually be expected to have a psychology-relevant masters degree. Ideally, your project should have been in a clinically related area and if either an academic or practising clinical psychologist supervised it, your project, and hence you, will look even better. A big plus is if the project findings are published or presented at a conference.

In addition, you are expected to have relevant experience. In part, that helps you to know what being a clinical psychologist involves. It's important to note that relevant experience can be gained before, during or after a degree and the more relevant experience you have, the better your application will appear. Relevant experience might be paid or unpaid, full-time or part-time, but should involve 'caring'. A very good example would be to work as an assistant in NHS departments of clinical psychology, but it would also be good, for example, to have worked with an eating disorders support group or with a child on the autistic spectrum. However, the more relevant the experience is to clinical psychology, the better. If you do not like the idea of working with different sorts of patient groups, then it is unlikely that you would enjoy being a clinical psychologist.

Box 9:2 Valuable Experience for a Clinical Psychology Student

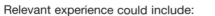

Relevant experience could include:

- working on a helpline
- helping out in an old people's home as an auxiliary care worker
- voluntary work with people with clinical problems
- working with a mental health charity
- shadowing a clinical psychologist.

It is always useful if you can work with a qualified clinical psychologist, particularly if they are prepared to be one of your referees. Admissions tutors for clinical psychology courses want applicants to know about clinical psychology, and that means working and talking with as many clinical psychologists as you can. But if your experience is obtained overseas, it is a good idea if you can also gain some experience working with the domestic system. If you are keen to attend a particular university, it is a good idea to ask the admissions tutor what would be the most appropriate relevant experience for applicants to their course.

You may be surprised to discover that research experience is also valued, particularly if the research is clinically related. You may be able to obtain research experience as part of work experience, by helping with a research study or by obtaining a post as a research assistant in a university or hospital. One way of gaining research experience is by working (probably unpaid, I'm afraid) over the summer with an academic, especially if they work in a clinically related area.

Advertisements for posts as 'assistant psychologist' or 'research assistant' are advertised in a variety of different ways. A good starting point is the BPS Appointments Memorandum, but also look on your psychology department's notice boards, or you may be lucky and have a department that emails vacancies to undergraduates. Good newspapers to read for job vacancies and articles on relevant jobs include the *Guardian* (*www.guardian.co.uk*), the *Independent* (www.independent.co.uk), *The Times* (www.times online.co.uk) and *The Times Higher Education Supplement* (www.thes.co.uk). It is worth checking out their online versions as some offer email alerts when suitable vacancies appear. Similarly, check out www.jobs.ac.uk for research-related jobs.

In the United Kingdom, funding for these courses is provided by the National Health Service (NHS). The relevant NHS Trust employs students as trainee clinical psychologists on a salary that is equivalent to a reasonable graduate starting salary. This means that students are employed by the NHS, so if you do not have the right to work in the United Kingdom, the NHS would have to apply for a work permit for you if you were offered a place. If you are not an applicant from the European Economic Area, you would not usually be considered for a clinical psychology course because the NHS is unlikely to employ anyone as a trainee clinical psychologist who needs a work permit to work in the United Kingdom.

Although clinical psychology has a reputation as being difficult to enter, if you are determined and are prepared to spend time gaining relevant experience, you should be in a very good position to get into clinical psychology.

Further information on courses in clinical psychology is available from the Clearing House for Postgraduate Courses in Clinical Psychology (www.leeds.ac.uk/chpccp). In the United Kingdom, you cannot apply directly to most universities offering clinical psychology. Instead, you apply through the Clearing House for a modest fee, indicating a maximum of four courses from over twenty for which you wish to be considered. All those courses lead to a doctoral level qualification and combine academic and practical training in a full-time three-year course. There are some universities that operate outside of the Clearing House, that is, University of Hertfordshire, University of Hull (undergraduate entry only) and Queen's University Belfast. In Ireland, University College Dublin (www.ucd.ie/~psydept/courses/doc_clinical.html) and Trinity College Dublin (www.tcd.ie/Psychology/clinical.html) offer clinical courses.

Further information:
The Clearing House
15 Hyde Terrace
Leeds LS2 9LT
Website: www.leeds.ac.uk/chpccp
Email: chpccp@leeds.ac.uk
Tel: 0113 343 2737
Fax: 0113 243 0908

Knight, A. (2002). *How to Become a Clinical Psychologist: Getting a Foot in the Door*. London: Brunner/Mazel.
Llewellyn, S. (1998). Clinical psychology training. *The Psychologist, 11*, 295.
Marzillier, J. and Hall, J. (Eds.). (1999). *What Is Clinical Psychology?* London: Oxford University Press.
Roth, A. D. (1998). Getting on clinical training courses. *The Psychologist, 11*, 589–92.

Psyclick (www.psyclick.org.uk). 'This site is a resource for anyone seeking to train as a clinical psychologist, particularly in the UK. It should be of interest to psychology undergraduates (or graduates), assistant psychologists, and anyone looking to find out more or get a "foot in the door"'.

Counselling psychology

What does a counselling psychologist actually *do*? Counselling psychologists work with clients to help them manage life events, such as the effects of childhood sexual abuse, bereavement, domestic violence and relationship breakdown. They also help people to deal with the symptoms of anxiety, depression, eating disorders and other psychological problems. They do this in partnership with the person they are counselling, working to empower them as part of an holistic approach that considers the context in which a person is experiencing problems. For example, someone suffering anxiety might have unresolved issues with forming relationships as a result of their childhood interactions within their family.

Counselling psychologists work in a variety of settings: general hospitals, psychiatric hospitals, GP surgeries, educational institutes, businesses, prisons and private practice. Indeed, some counselling psychologists work in a number of different settings, so they might be attached to a particular GP practice as well as seeing clients on a private basis. They typically work with individuals, but it is not unusual to work with couples, families and even groups of people.

The focus of most counselling psychology is providing psychological therapy. This usually involves assessing the problem and the wider context, identifying a psychological explanation (ideally with the client's active participation) and then planning and delivering psychological therapy.

In contrast to clinical psychology training, a BPS accredited post-graduate qualification in counselling psychology is not usually funded. However, universities offering post-graduate qualifications in counselling psychology should be able to provide information about sources of funding including research councils, charitable trusts, foundations and companies. Total costs excluding living costs are almost £3,000 per year and courses last three years. However, the pay scales are similar to clinical psychologists, so counselling psychology is another relatively well-paid profession.

Further information:

British Association for Counselling and Psychotherapy
BACP House
35–37 Albert Street
Rugby
Warks CV21 2SG
Website: www.bacp.co.uk
Email: bacp@bacp.co.uk
Tel: 0870 443 5252
Fax: 0870 443 5161

McLeod, J. (2003). *An Introduction to Counselling*. London: Open University Press.

The British Council has produced an excellent 'Subject Sheet' on psychology and counselling for those interested in studying psychology or counselling in the United Kingdom (www.britishcouncil.org/education/resource/infosheets/Psychology.pdf). It is aimed at non-UK nationals, but it is useful for British citizens too.

Educational psychology

What does an educational psychologist actually *do*? Educational psychologists work with young people in education to help them deal with learning difficulties and emotional or social problems. They write reports for teachers, children's panels or for court cases. Educational psychology can involve working directly with a child, monitoring their academic and personal development and providing counselling, or can involve working with primary caregivers and/or teachers. Most educational psychologists work within local education authorities, for social services departments, voluntary bodies and in nurseries, schools and colleges. Some work as independent private consultants.

To become an educational psychologist, you will need a first degree in psychology that provides GBR from the BPS. You then need to successfully complete a full-time three-year professional training course in educational psychology leading to a doctorate in educational psychology. Like clinical psychology there are funded training places with a 'salary' and fees paid. Qualified teachers who do not have a GBR-recognised psychology degree usually take a conversion course to obtain GBR-equivalence, and this is a popular route.

There is currently a shortage of qualified educational psychologists, but there is strong competition (similar to clinical psychology) for places on professional training. Local education authorities have created assistant educational psychologist posts to assist potential applicants in developing appropriate skills and experience. Post-graduate course applications for England and Wales should be made to the Clearing House for Postgraduate Courses in Educational Psychology. For Scotland, applications should be made directly to the appropriate university department.

Further information:

The Association of Educational Psychologists is the professional association and trade union for educational psychologists in the United Kingdom. Their academic journal, *Educational Psychology in Practice*, publishes papers that are likely to be of particular interest to educational psychologists, providing information and provoking debate on a wide range of professional issues.

The Association of Educational Psychologists
26 The Avenue
Durham DH1 4ED
Website: www.aep.org.uk
Email: N/A
Tel: 0191 384 9512
Fax: 0191 386 5287

The Clearing House for Postgraduate Courses in Educational Psychology
Employer's Organisation for local government
Layden House
76–86 Turnmill Street
London EC1M 5QU
Tel: 020 7296 6675
Website: www.lg-employers.gov.uk/skills/ed-psych/index.html

LTSN Psychology provides a list of resources on the Social Science Information Gateway (www.sosig.ac.uk/roads/subject-listing/World-cat/edupsych.html) that will give you a good idea of what is involved in educational psychology.

Forensic psychology

What does a forensic psychologist actually *do*? There is considerably less gambling, drinking and adulterous sex in the lives of *most* forensic psychologists than you might have expected from ITV's *Cracker* as played by Robbie Coltrane. Forensic psychologists do a variety of different tasks including: providing expert evidence in court, giving advice to mental health tribunals and parole boards, analysing crimes, devising and implementing treatment programmes, stress reduction for prisoners and prison staff, modifying behaviour of offenders and undertaking statistical analysis for prisoner profiling.

Forensic psychology is an increasingly popular area of psychology and demand for post-graduate qualifications is very high. To become a forensic psychologist, it is necessary to complete an accredited one-year full-time MSc in forensic psychology and complete stage 2 of the BPS's Diploma in forensic psychology. The stage 2 qualification involves supervised practice, which means that a chartered forensic psychologist supervises you over a two-year period. The exact requirements are set out in a 60-page BPS document (www. bps.org.uk/careers/forensic_diploma.cfm), but essentially the process involves assessing candidates on the range of competences that have been defined for forensic psychologists, using a portfolio containing a variety of evidence of their competence.

The largest employer of forensic psychologists is the prison service, but they are also found in the police service, the health service, private practice and in university psychology departments.

Further information:

'How to get on a forensic psychology course: your questions answered' (www.bps.org. uk/smg/formain.htm) is an invaluable resource produced by Andrew Silke, Centre for

Applied Psychology, University of Leicester. It answers questions such as: What is forensic psychology? How many places are available? How hard is it to get a place? What, then, are the various courses looking for when they review applications? What are the educational requirements? What if there is no forensic element to my under-graduate degree? How important is experience? Getting called for an interview. What questions will I be asked? Which is the 'best' course?

LTSN Psychology provides a list of resources on the Social Science Information Gateway (www.sosig.ac.uk/roads/subject-listing/World-cat/forensic.html) that will give you a good idea of what is involved in forensic psychology.

The Home Office has a website devoted to the prison service where there is information on psychology posts (www.hmprisonservice.gov.uk/careersandjobs/typeswork/psychologist).

Health psychology

What does a health psychologist actually *do*? A health psychologist uses psychological principles to devise ways to change people's attitudes and behaviours as well as the ways in which people think about health-related matters. The range of topics covered is extensive and includes such issues as health promotion (breast self-examination, testicular self-examination, exercise programmes, dental care and so on) and illness avoidance (safer sexual behaviour, smoking cessation and other addictions). In parti-cular, health psychologists are interested in promoting effective communication between health professionals and their clients to facilitate long-term changes in behav-iours. Health psychologists work within hospitals and health authorities as well as academic health research units and universities.

To become a health psychologist it is necessary to complete an accredited MSc in health psychology (one year full-time) plus completion of stage 2 qualification in health psychology. The stage 2 qualification involves supervised practice, which means that a chartered health psychologist supervises you over a two-year period. The exact require-ments are set out in a 69-page BPS document (www.bps.org.uk/careers/health_training. cfm), but essentially the process involves assessing candidates on the range of compe-tences that have been defined for health psychologists, using a portfolio containing a variety of evidence of their competence.

The field of health psychology is relatively new, so posts are not necessarily advertised as being for 'health psychologists'. Instead, reference is usually made to psychologists with relevant skills. However, it is likely that in the future specific posts for health psychologists will be advertised.

Further information:

Division of Health Psychology (DHP)
The British Psychological Society
St Andrews House
48 Princess Road East
Leicester LE1 7DR
Website: www.health-Psychology.co.uk
Email: enquiry@bps.org.uk
Tel: 0116 254 9568
Fax: 0116 247 0787

The DHP website contains useful information such as BPS accredited MSc courses in health psychology as well as details of studentships and post-qualification jobs. There is also information about the British REsearch And Training in HEalth Psychology initiative (BREATHE), which is allied with the BPS division of health psychology, and sets out to promote training and collaboration for early career researchers in health psychology. BREATHE provides training workshops to those at an early stage in their health psychology career, as well as providing a resource/support network for early career researchers in health psychology. If you think a career in health psychology might suit you, you could check out the Health Psychology Postgraduate Network (www.jiscmail.ac.uk/lists/HEALTH-PSYCH.html) to see if you are interested in the topics that are discussed.

Neuropsychology

What does a neuropsychologist actually *do?* In essence, neuropsychologists are concerned with assessment and rehabilitation of those who have suffered some sort of brain damage due to stroke, brain trauma, brain infection, brain tumours or a neurodegenerative disorder. Neuropsychologists work in neuroscience centres alongside neurosurgeons, neurologists and associated medical professionals, providing post-trauma assessment, training and support as part of a multidisciplinary team in rehabilitation centres and community centres. In addition, neuropsychologists act as expert witnesses in court cases, usually for personal injury claims.

The BPS has recently raised the level of training required to be a recognised neuropsychologist. The following paragraph is slightly modified from the BPS website:

> To be a Practitioner Full Member, you must have first established your professional competence in a related field of applied psychology (usually, but not exclusively, in clinical psychology) sufficient to be eligible to be a chartered psychologist. You must then have gained

the equivalent of two year's full-time experience working in clinical neuropsychological practice. You also need to satisfy assessors that you have worked under appropriate supervision and met the approved standard by the submission of case studies and research reports. You must also satisfy the examiners in four examinations relating to the underpinning knowledge for clinical neuropsychological practice. This qualification therefore sets a high standard for clinical practice, and Practitioner Full Members of the Division will have undertaken a minimum of eight years of training from first entering into psychology; the normal period of study will more commonly be 10 to 12 years.

Further information:

The BPS Division of Neuropsychology is the best starting point as you can see the latest information on the development of this profession (www.bps.org.uk).

LTSN Psychology provides a list of resources on the Social Science Information Gateway (www.sosig.ac.uk/roads/subject-listing/World-cat/physneuro.html) that will give you a good idea of what is involved in neuropsychology.

Also worth checking out is www.neuropsychology.co.uk, which provides information for all neuropsychologists, but with an emphasis on those working or studying in Britain. In particular, there is information on jobs and studentships in neuropsychology. The American equivalent is Neuropsychology Central (www.neuropsychologycentral.com).

Occupational psychology

What does an occupational psychologists actually *do*? Occupational psychologists are also known as work and organisational psychologists and those different names give a good indication of what they do. They are concerned with how organisations work and how people work within those organisations, both as individuals and as groups. The intention is to improve the functioning of an organisation and, hopefully, increase individuals' job satisfaction. An occupational psychologist may be involved with 'monitoring recruitment processes, training, evaluation and assisting workers in transitioning from employment to a non-employed state'. Otherwise, an occupational psychology might help an organisation develop a new culture, teach skills useful to an organisation and assist in industrial relations.

Occupational psychologists work for large organisations (both public and private), but particularly within the Civil Service. In the private sector, salaries *can* reach six figures!

Much of what an occupational psychologist does also comes under the term of 'personnel' or 'human resources' and it is possible to go straight into that area after graduation. Maturity is valued within this profession and it is not unusual to take post-graduate qualifications while in work. To become chartered, you need to take an accredited one-year full-time MSc in occupational psychology followed by two years of supervised work experience.

Further information:

Chartered Institute of Personnel and Development
CIPD House
Camp Road
Wimbledon
London SW19 4UX
Website: www.cipd.co.uk
Email: N/A
Tel: 020 8971 9000
Fax: 020 8263 3333

LTSN Psychology provides a list of resources on the Social Science Information Gateway (www.sosig.ac.uk/roads/subject-listing/World-cat/indpsych.html) that will give you a good idea of what is involved in occupational psychology.

Sports psychology

What does a sports psychologist actually *do*? Sports psychologists work in a wide variety of situations. There are sports psychologists who provide assistance to national and local teams in football, rugby and cricket as well as in other sports. Similarly, individual sportspeople, such as tennis players, may use a sports psychologist. These sports psychologists apply their knowledge of psychology to enhance performance in sport, diagnosing problems and developing ways of addressing those problems (such as 'choking' in golf where nerves can become a problem in competitive play). Other sports psychologists are more similar to health psychologists (and may even be chartered health psychologists) and are concerned with encouraging sport, exercise and physical activity for the benefits to psychological and physical health.

Sports psychology is appealing, like many careers in psychology, because it involves helping others, usually as part of a team, but also because it offers a diverse range of experiences where you can see the results of your hard work, maybe even in the form of an Olympic gold medal or a national or international cup competition. However, there are fewer career opportunities, the salaries are generally not particularly good, the hours can be long depending on the client, and burnout is common due to the pressure of working in a stressful environment. That said, being a sports psychologist can be incredibly satisfying and rewarding.

The BPS website states that:

> In March 2004, the Division of Sport and Exercise Psychology was formed which, for the first time in the United Kingdom, makes it possible for an individual to qualify as a chartered sport and exercise psychologist. As the Division is still in its very early stages, formal training routes have yet to be defined. The qualifications are likely to include:
>
> - An accredited undergraduate degree that confers the Graduate Basis for Registration.
> - An approved higher degree in psychology or sport and exercise psychology.
> - A specified length of quality supervised experience.

Further information:

British Association of Sport and Exercise Sciences
Chelsea Close
Off Amberley Road
Armley
Leeds LS12 4HP
Website: www.bases.org.uk
Email: jbairstow@bases.org.uk
Tel: 0113 289 1010
Fax: 0113 289 1020

LTSN Psychology provides a list of resources on the Social Science Information Gateway (www.sosig.ac.uk/roads/subject-listing/World-cat/sportleis.html) that will give you a good idea of what is involved in sports psychology.

Teaching and research in psychology

What does an academic psychologist actually *do*? Deliver a few lectures, do a little marking and go down the pub. Or at least that seems to be the view of some students! Most academic psychologists work as lecturers, but giving lectures is often the smallest parts of their jobs. Instead, lecturers usually spend their time doing three things: research, teaching and administration (and writing books like this). Given the pressure on their time, most academics work evenings and weekends and use the vacations to attend conferences and write papers, as well as prepare materials for the next term. Oh, and the salary is pretty poor too. So why would anyone do this? Lecturers usually have a greater degree of flexibility with their time and work to largely self-imposed deadlines. Some particularly enjoy the thrill of teaching, explaining difficult concepts so that their audience can understand them; others enjoy the thrill of discovery, understanding behaviour and the way organisms work, and others enjoy doing research that could empower and improve the lives of disadvantaged people.

Some lecturers are already chartered in other fields such as health psychology and mix the usual lecturing activities with continuing their applied discipline, often directly combining that practice with research. Another option is to work solely as a researcher (often in research centres), but that is relatively rare.

To become an academic psychologist, you would usually do a PhD (at least three-years full-time) with perhaps a relevant MSc beforehand. Increasingly, universities are requiring newly appointed lecturing staff to complete a Postgraduate Certificate in Higher Education (PGCHE). To do a PhD, you need two things: a supervisor willing to supervise you, and funding. To find a supervisor, you need to consider issues such as in what area you wish to research and are there any limitations on where you could study. Remember that a supervisor makes a substantial commitment when they agree to supervise a student, so they will want to be sure that you are capable and committed. If you fail to complete your PhD, that fact reflects badly on the supervisor. Once you have a supervisor you need to obtain funding. Rarely, your supervisor might have access to funding, either because they have a funded research project or they might have access to department funds to support a PhD student. Otherwise, the usual source of funds is the research councils, mainly the Economic and Social Research Council (www.esrc.ac.uk), the Medical Research Council (www.mrc.ac.uk) and the Biotechnology and Biological Sciences Research Council (www.bbsrc.ac.uk). In addition, some charities support PhD studentships (for example, Leverhulme Trust, www.leverhulme.org.uk) and some companies are prepared to fund, at least, partially a PhD studentship. Otherwise, there is the option to self-fund, but that costs almost £30,000 in total (at the time of writing). It is best to talk to your potential supervisor as soon as possible about funding options for doing a PhD with them in their institution.

Further information:

This is one career where your academic staff really should be very helpful and they are the best starting point. If you speak to someone who teaches/researches in the field in which you are interested, they should be able to identify potential supervisors. You should then look at the website for that institution.

You can check university psychology departments in Britain and Ireland at www.Psychology.bangor. ac.uk/links/BIPsychDepts

Psychotherapy

Psychotherapy is an interesting case; most people without a background in psychology would think that psychologists are actually psychotherapists. However, psychotherapy is a *very* diverse discipline and the BPS has struggled with a way to acknowledge psychologists with expertise in psychotherapy (the BPS refers to a 'century of "tribal" disputes between different "schools" and "models"'). In March 2004, the BPS launched its 'Register of Psychologists Specialising in Psychotherapy' for psychologists already chartered, but who have achieved basic competence in psychotherapy.

It is worth stating here the six principles that indicate what is expected from psychologists specialising in psychotherapy as this is seen as a template for other specialist registers that may follow, for example, sports psychology. The six principles are (BPS, 2004):

1. **Active recognition of the necessary interplay between psychological and psychotherapeutic theory, knowledge and practice.**

2. **The fundamental importance of ongoing inquiry in psychology and psychotherapy.**

3. **The need to develop understanding, knowledge and practical competence in psychotherapy.**

4. **The requirement for continuing personal development and supervision in relation to psychotherapy practice.**

5. **The importance of wider social, cultural and political knowledge and awareness in relation to psychotherapy.**

6. **The necessity for continuing professional development to meet the requirements of periodic re-registration as psychologists specialising in psychotherapy.**

So, what does a psychotherapist actually *do*? 'Tell me about your childhood. Tell me about your dreams.' Most people have not had psychotherapy, but think they have a good idea of what is involved in psychotherapy. The psychotherapist is an elderly, bearded man who talks in a middle-European accent while the client lies on a sofa talking about their childhood, their dreams, their relations to their parents, their fantasies and so on. Well, it *can* be like that, but psychotherapy is an enormous area with many different theoretical perspectives. Psychotherapy can be best thought of as similar to counselling psychology in terms of what they actually do, but psychotherapists usually have very specific theoretical backgrounds and as a result very different kinds of training. For example, a Freudian analyst would have been in weekly therapy for a number of years before practising.

The United Kingdom Council for Psychotherapists (UKCP) has eight sections that represent different approaches to psychotherapy:

1. analytical psychology

2. behavioural and cognitive psychotherapies

3. experiential constructivist therapies

4. family, couple, sexual and systemic therapy

5. humanistic and integrative psychotherapy

6. hypno-psychotherapy

7. psychoanalytic and psychodynamic

8. psychoanalytically based therapy with children.

Entry requirements for training for all eight sections include: entry at post-graduate level of competence; personal qualities that make you suitable for the profession of psychotherapy; and relevant experience of working with people in a responsible role. Training must be at post-graduate level and will not normally be shorter than four years part-time duration (or equivalent).

The UKCP advises that if you want to pursue training in psychotherapy you will need to find out about the different kinds of psychotherapy, or 'modalities' as they are described at UKCP, and think about what interests and attracts you. Some of the questions you might ask yourself include:

What kind of psychotherapist do I want to be?

Do I want to be a hypnotherapist or a humanistic psychotherapist?

Do I want to be a behavioural or an analytic psychotherapist?

Do I want to work with individuals or couples or families or groups?

Do I want to work privately or within the NHS?

If you are unsure about the kind of psychotherapist you want to train as, or what setting you hope to work in, then you need to do some reading about the different approaches.

Further information:

The British Confederation for Psychotherapists (BCP)
West Hill House
6 Swains Lane
London N6 6QS
Website: www.bcp.org.uk
Email: mail@bcp.org.uk
Tel: 020 7267 3626
Fax: 020 7267 4772

United Kingdom Council for Psychotherapists (UKCP)
167–169 Great Portland Street
London W1W 5PF
Website: www.psychotherapy.org.uk
Email: ukcp@psychotherapy.org.uk
Tel: 020 7436 3002
Fax: 020 7436 3013

Opportunities Outside the United Kingdom

Some countries have very specific rules about working as a psychologist. Indeed, in Europe most countries have legislation governing who is legally entitled to call himself or herself a psychologist. The United Kingdom is unusual in not having such legislation, and the BPS is working hard for such statutory legislation and it is expected that such legislation will be brought into law soon.

Europe (EU and non-EU)

There are opportunities for those with British psychology qualifications to work outside the United Kingdom. Qualifications and training obtained in the United Kingdom are still respected all over the world. If you are a citizen of the European Union, you can work in any country in the European Economic Area. However, it is likely that you will need the appropriate language skills and may need to have your qualifications and experience recognised by the appropriate national psychological organisation. If you are interested in working in a particular country, it is best to contact the national psychology association of that country as a first step so that they can tell you if you will be able to practise there as a psychologist, as well as informing you of the best places to look for advertised posts. You can find contact details for all European psychology associations (including those countries not in the European Union) via the European Federation of Psychologists' Associations (www.efpa.be).

Outside Europe

Outside Europe, whether or not you can work as a psychologist in a particular country will depend on the rules and regulations in that country. The best starting point is the American Psychologists Association website (www.apa.org) as it contains an impressive contact list of national psychologist associations as well as subject-specific psychology organisations. Once you have contacted the relevant national psychological association, it is a *very* good idea to contact a psychologist in your field working in that country to see what their working conditions are like and to discover the status of psychologists in that country. The national psychological association might be able to help you make that contact.

Completing Applications

There is a huge amount of information available both in book form and on the Internet on completing application forms and, in particular, producing curricula vitae (CVs). However, there are some key ideas that you should bear in mind:

- **NEVER lie – you *will* be caught out eventually.**

- **Follow the instructions accurately.**

- **Get someone else to check your grammar and punctuation.**

- **Keep things clear and simple.**

- **Show how *your* experiences have helped you address their questions.**

- **Get someone in the relevant area to look at your completed application.**

You should carefully read the application form and in particular any guidance notes to ensure that you are presenting yourself in the best possible light *for that particular vacancy*. Normally for a job vacancy you will be given an explicit job description with bullet points of the specific skills required. In your application, you need to ensure that you have addressed each of those points, but do so explicitly with appropriate examples. For example, rather than just writing 'I am numerate', it is better to write 'I am numerate, as demonstrated by my consistently good marks in research methods and statistics and my extensive use of quantitative data in my project.' It is always a good idea to include a brief covering letter that highlights how you meet the requirements of the job description.

Again, use our OCR idea. For every separate application, you need to organise whatever is required (including checking with your referees that they will be available to write you a reference). You need to ensure that you communicate *relevant* information for that *particular* application. It is useful to have a standard CV that you can use quickly and which you constantly update. It is always a good idea to tailor the content and perhaps the order so that you highlight your skills, experiences and qualifications to respond accurately to the requirements of the vacancy. After each application, reflect on what you did. If you had an interview, think about what went well and what didn't. If you didn't get an interview, review your entire application to see if there was anything that you could have done differently.

Conclusion

Psychology as a career path is relatively young. However, it is clear that the demand for psychological services is steadily increasing and that there is growing recognition, both within health services and society as a whole, that psychological issues need to be addressed. As a result, the opportunities for a psychologist are likely to continue to expand, making a career in psychology an excellent choice.

Box 9:3   Before You Move On ...

Where can you get information on careers in psychology?

What careers are available outside psychology to graduates in psychology?

What is involved in doing clinical psychology?

What is involved in doing counselling psychology?

What is involved in doing educational psychology?

What is involved in doing forensic psychology?

What is involved in doing health psychology?

What is involved in doing neuropsychology?

What is involved in doing occupational psychology?

What is involved in doing teaching and research in psychology?

What is involved in doing sports psychology?

What is involved in doing psychotherapy?

If you're looking at this appendix:

- **You are a prospective student who wants to study psychology.**

- **You have decided that you have chosen the wrong psychology course and want to study psychology elsewhere.**

- **You are someone who wants reassurance that you have chosen the right course for *you*.**

How do I Choose a Psychology Degree that's Most Appropriate for Me?

If you are looking for universities that offer psychology, your first step is to look at the University Central Admissions Service (UCAS) website (www.ucas.com). You may be surprised to find that there are nearly 100 institutions that offer degrees in psychology. But how do you decide which course to choose? Here are some questions you might find helpful to consider:

- **Does the degree confer 'GBR' from the British Psychological Society?**

- **What is important for choosing my university:**

    - **Geographical location?**

    - **Prestige?**

    - **The nature of the teaching and assessments?**

    - **Facilities?**

Box A:1 Do You Already Have a Degree, But Not in Psychology?

If you are a graduate who has maybe worked for a few years, but want a change of career into psychology, you do not need to complete a full psychology degree. Instead, you can take a conversion qualification (normally either a graduate diploma or masters qualification) to gain GBR. These courses normally take one or two years full-time or up to four years part-time. Details of conversion courses are available on the BPS website (www.bps.org.uk).

Alternatively, you can take the BPS qualifying examination, which has papers covering the main areas of psychology. However, it is unlikely that you would succeed in passing that exam unless you had studied a number of psychology units at university level.

Choosing a Specific Degree at a Specific University

People's priorities differ. You may want to be at a nearby university so you can live at home while you do your degree. You may want to go to the most prestigious university you can and are not too concerned about the location of the university, the content of the degree or the way it is taught. However, whatever your priorities, you need to consider where you want to study and identify the right university and psychology department for you.

Is geographical location important to you?

There are universities scattered all through the country in the United Kingdom. You might be particularly keen to attend university in an urban area, wanting to enjoy a particular scene (dance, lesbian/gay and so on), or you may definitely *not* want to live in a dirty, grimy, expensive city and would much prefer a more rural setting, or you may prefer somewhere in between. The important thing to realise is that what is right has to be right for you. We love living in a dirty, grimy and expensive city (London) as we enjoy theatre, art, public talks and the diversity of people. That means London is the right choice for *us*, but it is easy to imagine people who would find living in London to be their worst nightmare. It is best to try to talk to people who have experience of the different places that you are considering. However, you have to remember that people's opinions (like ours) will inevitably be biased.

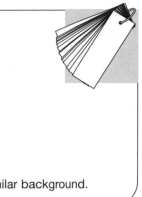

Box A:2   Choosing a University

Some factors that *might* be relevant for you when choosing
a university:

- big city vs. countryside
- coastal vs. inland
- able to live on campus vs. most students live off campus
- one unitary campus vs. sites spread across an area
- diverse student population vs. students mostly from a similar background.

One good strategy is to look at the wide range of student guides that are available. Some of the material is actually available online (particularly for the newspaper guides), but remember that the information will be out of date *before* it is even published. Always check out important information. If you want to attend a particular university because it has an Olympic-size swimming pool, check that the pool is actually still open! The best thing you can do when you have narrowed down your options to, say four or five, is to take advantage of any open days held by those universities.

We would suggest looking at a couple of these books in your local bookshop and consider buying one that has the information that seems most relevant to you:

Dudgeon, P. (Ed.). (2006). *The Virgin 2007 Alternative Guide to British Universities*. London: Virgin Books.
Hindmarsh, A., Kingston, B., O'Leary, J. (Eds.). (2006). *The 'Times' Good University Guide*. London: Time Books.
Leach, J. (Ed.). (2006). *'Guardian' University Guide*: *Where to go, what to study, how to get there*. London: Guardian Newspapers Ltd.

One book that you might find particularly useful with its listing of the point scores required for entry into every course is:

Heap, B. (2006). *Degree Course Offers – 2007 Entry: The Comprehensive Guide on Entry to Universities and Colleges*. London: Trotman.

Another useful book that is explicitly about entry to psychology degrees is:

Burnett, J. and Waterstone, M. (2006). *Getting into Psychology*. London: Trotman.

Entry requirements for psychology degrees

Universities differ in the precise entry requirements that they have for their psychology degrees. All will usually require you to have at least two A-levels (or equivalent) and GCSEs in English language and mathematics, but the precise requirements will differ from university to university. It is worth finding out about a university's entry requirements before you submit your UCAS application, since you do not want to apply to a university that requires, say, 21 A-level points when you are only likely to achieve, say, 12 A-level points. Universities will publicise their normal entry requirements in their prospectus, and you can ask admissions tutors for precise details of a particular department's requirements.

'Point scores? I don't have A-levels. Help!'.

Don't worry if you do not have A-levels or Scottish highers. If you are over 21, you count as a mature student and universities are allowed to accept you on to a degree course on the basis of relevant prior learning or experience. That could mean that you have completed a programme of study since school or have experience of working in a caring profession, for example as a care assistant. Usually, the admissions tutor will want to feel confident that you will be able to handle the burden of making use of lectures and seminars, studying independently and writing essays and practical reports. Therefore, you might have to attend an interview, write an essay under timed conditions or simply bring along some work that you have completed in your own time. Remember that this process is for *your* benefit too, as no one benefits when someone who is not suited for a degree attempts to study for one.

Sometimes, the admissions tutor may recommend that you first take a foundation or access course. Foundation courses are offered by universities and usually guarantee a place on a degree course if they are successfully completed. Access courses are usually offered by further education colleges and are a recognised means of entry to university degrees. Although it means delaying a degree for a year, both of these are a good opportunity for you to find out if you would really enjoy doing a university degree without making a three-year commitment. If you choose a good foundation or access course, you may even find yourself at an advantage compared to students coming straight from school or college.

Finally, remember that although psychology is a very popular degree course and entry can be very competitive at certain institutions, there are always places available somewhere in the country, particularly if you are over 21.

Choosing a Psychology Department

Once you have chosen a geographical area (such as a big city like London or Manchester), the next obvious step is to choose a university. Well, yes and no. Although you will study for your degree at a particular university, you really study for your degree with a particular department. You should try to focus on the psychology department rather than the university in which it is located.

Box A:3   Possible Questions You Might Ask when Considering a Specific Psychology Department

Does the degree offered have the Graduate Basis for Registration?

Do you want to study in a large psychology department or a small psychology department?

Does the department have masters courses and a PhD programme?

What laboratory facilities does the department have?

What are the entry requirements and what was the minimum standard that was actually accepted last year?

Is it possible to change from full-time study to part-time study during the degree?

Does the department have any teaching material on their website? If so, do you like the look of the material?

What is the emphasis of the degree – biological or more social? Both are fine, but you might have a preference for one over the other.

What final year options are currently available and are there any restrictions?

Does teaching take place on one campus or do you have to travel between campuses? Having to travel between campuses can make your time at university more complicated.

Who actually teaches the degree? A department may have famous psychologists, but they are unlikely to have become famous for their undergraduate teaching! It is possible that they do not actually teach at all on the undergraduate degree.

What is the assessment pattern? Are there lots of examinations or is the emphasis on coursework?

Is there any information about guidelines on the return of work?

Are there policies on what feedback you can expect to receive and when you can expect to see it?

Can the department give you an indicative timetable for the first year?

What is the nature of the tutorial support provided by the department? For example, do academic staff have dedicated tutorial hours?

Does the department meet your specific needs? (Are you a parent/guardian? Do you have a disability of some kind?)

A number of newspapers have started to produce league tables of universities (for example, *The Times* www.thetimes.co.uk) and some have even produced league tables of psychology departments (for example, the *Guardian*, www.guardian.co.uk). These can be unpopular with academics, particularly with those at institutions that are low in the tables. While these tables can be useful, they need to be handled with care. The main problem is that there are no clear criteria about what would constitute a good university and how to combine those criteria. Indeed, producing a scale to allow ranking on a measure is one of the skills that you may develop as part of your psychology degree.

Normally, the league tables take account of teaching scores, research scores, percentage employment of graduates, staff:student ratios, money spent per student, and average point scores of entrants. While these are useful measures on their own, it is not clear how they are combined to give one ranking. The source data are sometimes inaccurate, as they require assumptions on how money is distributed and the data are usually out of date. Most disturbing is how relatively small changes on one factor can drastically alter the position of an institution. A good illustration of this problem is when our university spent millions of pounds on a new learning resources centre containing hundreds of computers and other kinds of electronic learning aids. Unfortunately, one newspaper decided that such expenditure did not count as library expenditure as it was not for books! As a result, our institution fell over ten places in their league table! So, do have a look at the tables, but focus more on individual components and ask yourself how they relate to you.

Another source of information is reports produced by the Quality Assurance Agency (QAA), who visit and 'inspect' the quality of provision in each subject area in each university every five years. The reports are freely available on the QAA's website (www. qaa.ac.uk). These reports can provide useful information but, as with league tables, they must be read with care. In particular, they are a 'snapshot' of the quality of provision at a specific time (so they may well be very out of date), and even where the visits have taken place close to when you apply you should be aware that universities respond quickly to rectify weaknesses that are identified.

Do you want to combine your study of psychology with another subject?

Most universities that offer degrees in psychology also offer it as a 'field' of a combined honours degree. Usually that means that you study equal amounts of psychology and another topic subject in the first year and then in the remaining years you either study equal amounts of each field or concentrate on one – the major – while still studying the other – the minor. It is also sometimes possible to transfer over completely to one of those fields at the end of the *second* year of study, but you must check with each specific institution before starting to see what their rules allow. These degrees can still qualify for GBR, but usually only for the major and joint pathways where the final year project is in psychology.

Some students choose to do combined honours psychology as a career decision. For example, psychology is not currently a national curriculum subject, so if you wanted to do teacher training after you graduate it might be best to study psychology with a national curriculum subject like English. Then you would be able to do a Postgraduate Certificate in Education (PGCE) and still be able, ultimately, to become a chartered educational psychologist, as long as your degree qualifies for GBR.

If you follow the path we have outlined you should soon have a number of possible institutions where you might like to study. The next step is to visit them either before or after you apply. While you might get the chance to visit when you are interviewed, many institutions no longer use interviews as a major part of their admissions procedure. But most universities will hold open days. you should find out if there is a psychology-specific open day rather than a general open day, as you should find psychology staff at the former but not necessarily at the latter. In particular, you should try to see the laboratory facilities, library facilities, computer facilities and rooms used for teaching and perhaps even the accommodation. If the place seems dirty and depressing, it is sensible to avoid it as three years of doom and gloom is not going to help you to get a good degree and is unlikely to produce upbeat, inspiring staff.

I have Special Needs – is there Anything Specific I Should Do?

Special needs can include students with dyslexia, partial-sight, mobility difficulties and other needs that mean those students require different support from other students. The recently passed Disability Act states that for universities:

> It is unlawful for the body responsible for an educational institution to discriminate against a disabled person:
>
> (a)   in the arrangements it makes for determining admissions to the institution;
> (b)   in the terms on which it offers to admit him to the institution; or
> (c)   by refusing or deliberately omitting to accept an application for his admission to the institution. [Gender-specific language in the original legislation.]

You might think that the Disability Act means that universities will therefore automatically provide the assistance that you require, but sadly that is not really true as provision varies dramatically between universities. The best first step is to contact the admissions tutor and gauge their attitude from their responses to your questions on how they would be able to support you. In particular, ask if you can have an appointment with their disabilities support unit to see how your needs may be met. If you are dissatisfied, then you may want to go elsewhere. If you are particularly keen on a specific institution, but are concerned that their support might not be as good as it ought to be, remember that universities hate bad publicity!

Index